Real World Resea

Developing a Questionnaire 2nd Edition

DATE DUE

Also available from Continuum

Real World Research Series

Case Study Research Methods, Bill Gillham

The Research Interview, Bill Gillham

Observation Methods: Structured to Unstructured, Bill Gillham

Small-scale Social Survey Methods, Bill Gillham

Also available

Questionnaire Design, Interviewing and Attitude Measurement, A.N. Oppenheim

Developing a Questionnaire 2nd Edition

Bill Gillham

continuum

300
Gillham

Continuum International Publishing Group
The Tower Building   80 Maiden Lane, Suite 704
11 York Road   New York, NY 10038
London SE1 7NX
www.continuumbooks.com

© Bill Gillham 2007

First published 2000
Reprinted 2002 (twice), 2004 (twice), 2008

British Library Cataloguing-in-Publication Data
A catalogue record for this book is available from the British Library.

ISBN: 9780826496317 (paperback)

Typeset by YHT Ltd, London
Printed and bound in Great Britain by
Antony Rowe Ltd, Chippenham, Wiltshire

Contents

Series Foreword   vii

Acknowledgements   ix

1   The Pros and Cons of Questionnaires   1

2   Preparation   15

3   Drafting the Questions (and Answers)   25

4   Designing the Questionnaire   37

5   Getting Them Out and Getting Them Back   45

6   Displaying the Results for Analysis   49

7   Content Analysis of Open Questions   63

8   Statistical Analysis of Closed Questions   71

9   The Use of Questionnaires in Surveys   81

10 The Face-to-Face Questionnaire: Recording
    Schedules   87

11 Using Questionnaires in Telephone Interviews   93

12 Questionnaires as Part of a Multi-method
    Approach   99

13 Presenting Your Findings   103

Contents

Recommended Further Reading 107

Index 109

Series Foreword

The success of the first books in this series was encouraging but not entirely surprising. Research is a practical activity and few methods titles, even relatively advanced ones, are sufficiently practical at the level of useable detail. And those hefty, apparently comprehensive 'introductory' tomes – dispiriting to students – are usually only adequate for writing exam answers: hardly an end in itself.

A further limitation of existing texts is that they tend to present a prescription impossible within the constraints of a modest research project in a real-world setting. Or, indeed in anything less than an ideal world. Like any other engagement with reality, research is often a matter of making the best compromise that none the less preserves the essential values of a disciplined investigation.

Bill Gillham

Acknowledgements

Mrs Jane Cuthill produced the successive drafts of the manuscript with a speed and skill I have come to take for granted. My wife Judith polished the writing and corrected lapses of taste.

Postgraduate students at the University of Strathclyde and the Glasgow School of Art made demands that led me to clarify my thinking and not take too much for granted.

1

The Pros and Cons of Questionnaires

It is easy to construct a questionnaire. With a word processor it is possible to put together in an evening something that looks quite respectable. After all, we know what questionnaires look like: hardly a week goes by without some such coming our way.

Journalists often make them up (the term is exact) to fill in space in a magazine, with titles such as 'Are You A Party Bore?' or 'Judge Your Own Social Class'. They may be quite amusing to fill in and no one takes them seriously, least of all their originators. But many so-called 'research' questionnaires are put together in a no more impressive fashion.

Yet developing a questionnaire that will yield worthwhile data is difficult. And it has to be said here that the quality of the data emerging from even an adequately developed questionnaire is not wonderful. More on that later. The essential point is that good research cannot be built on poorly collected data; and even if the data are intended for nothing more than the oblivion of a master's degree dissertation, everything that follows from them is unsound. As a basis for practical action, poorly collected data will be wasteful of time and money, and discredit the name of 'research'.

The great popularity of questionnaires is that they provide a 'quick fix' for research methodology; no single method has been so much abused. This is a pity, because questionnaires have their place as one method, of most value when used in tandem with other methods. This *multi-method* approach to real-life questions is important, because one approach is rarely adequate; and if the results of different methods converge (agree, or fit together) then we can have greater confidence in the findings.

Why questionnaires?

Questionnaires are just one of a range of ways of getting information from people (or answers to our research questions), usually by posing direct or indirect questions. Incidentally, one of the weaknesses of questionnaires is that they seek to get answers *just* by asking questions. Table 1.1 presents this range schematically; this needs to be studied before you read on.

From Table 1.1 you can see that questionnaires are at the 'structured' end of the continuum. By this is meant that the researcher determines the questions that are asked and the range of answers that can be given. Of course, the 'respondent' has a choice; *yes/no, agree/disagree*, ticking one answer out of four or five, and so on. But the researcher has already decided on the possible answers: all he or she wants to find out is *which* answers are selected. This makes it very tidy for the researcher and easy to analyse. It can also be boring and frustrating for the respondent, although this depends to some extent on the amount of development work the researcher put into the questionnaire before it was distributed.

However, it is obvious that if all the questions and all the possible answers are determined in advance, the element of discovery is much reduced (unless there is a very unexpected pattern to the answers selected). You don't know what lies behind the responses selected or, more importantly, answers the respondents might have given had they been free to respond as they wished. It is partly for this reason that

Table 1.1 The verbal data dimension

Unstructured						Structured
Listening to other people's conversation; a kind of verbal observation	Using 'natural' conversation to ask research questions	'Open-ended' interviews; just a few key open questions, e.g. 'elite interviewing'	Semi-structured interviews, i.e. open and closed questions	Recording schedules: in effect, verbally administered questionnaires	Semi-structured questionnaires: multiple choice and open questions	Structured questionnaires: simple, specific, closed questions

questionnaire data are necessarily superficial: you only have the answers to go on.

More or less structure

For most people doing small-scale research in their spare time, the most unstructured methods are impractical. But sociologists and social anthropologists who want to find out how different cultures (or sub-cultures) work have to use these methods. In doing so they immerse themselves in the 'alien' culture: they look and they listen, and they sometimes ask questions. The formal structure of an interview or questionnaire would be both unacceptable and intrusive, as well as practically impossible. In the street culture of Chicago or Liverpool, as in the river tribes of the Amazon, the artificiality of such methods is staringly obvious. But that should make us reflect on the constraints that such methods impose anyway. Interviews and questionnaires are self-conscious things. Are the answers you are getting what people really think? When teachers fill in a questionnaire at the end of an in-service training course do they say the same things as they do in the informal atmosphere of the staffroom? Answers that are given as a result of the method used are *artefacts* of that method.

In short, there is a tension here: between the originality and discovery and validity of the verbal data, and the economy of time and effort and money in gathering the data. The only answer is a compromise; but that compromise has to be kept in mind.

Open and closed questions

What these terms means can be inferred from what has gone before but, to make the distinction explicit, a *closed* question is one where the possible answers are predetermined. Most questionnaires (and structured interviews) are composed entirely of closed questions. A very simple example is: *Which of the following newspapers do you read at least once a week?* (followed by a suitable list). Sometimes there is an 'other' category as well. An *open* question version of this is: *Which newspapers do you read at least once a week?* (where the respondent has to think and write in the answers). Here, where the answer is a factual one and fairly predictable, a closed question is probably better. But when the answers are in terms of opinions, beliefs or judgements, a small range of answers is much less likely to be representative. More than that, researchers commonly find themselves resorting to techniques that force responses into predetermined categories.

Open questions are only occasionally used in questionnaires because they are more difficult to analyse (and more troublesome to answer). However, we should note here that careful semi-structured interviewing *prior* to the questionnaire being constructed can mean that most of the probable answers are identified.

I argue below that open questions can lead to a greater level of discovery but that their number and kind has to be restricted to justify the 'cost'.

For and against questionnaires

In research we have to balance the gains and losses in anything we choose to do. Boxes 1 and 2 summarize the pros and cons of questionnaires. As you run your eye down the list in Box 1 (overleaf) it seems to present an unarguable case. Let us take each point in turn.

1. *Low cost in time and money.* This is the overwhelming argument. You can send out a thousand questionnaires

5

Box 1 For questionnaires

> - Low cost in time and money.
> - Easy to get information from a lot of people very quickly.
> - Respondents can complete the questionnaire when it suits them.
> - Analysis of answers to closed questions is straightforward.
> - Less pressure for an immediate response.
> - Respondents' anonymity.
> - Lack of interviewer bias.
> - Standardization of questions (but true of structured interviews).
> - Can provide suggestive data for testing an hypothesis.

in the time it takes to do two semi-structured interviews. And pro rata the financial costs of mailing questionnaires are minuscule compared with the probable travelling costs, both in time and money, involved in interviewing. Telephone interviewing (now more common) cuts out the travelling but is still very time-consuming. The main saving in the use of questionnaires is in time, not money, and for those doing research in addition to a full-time job that can be a critical factor.

2. *Easy to get information from a lot of people very quickly.* If it is efficiently organized, responses to even a large-scale questionnaire can be pulled in within a matter of weeks. The number of interviews one could hope to complete in that time would be little more than a handful (the people you want to interview may not be readily available or may be unwilling to be interviewed when you *do* contact them).

3. *Respondents can complete the questionnaire when it suits them.* Interviewing can be a complicated business as far as finding mutually convenient times is concerned. But you can just leave a questionnaire for someone to complete when he or she has the time.

4. *Analysis of answers to closed questions is relatively straightforward.* You can in fact have your analysis sheets (see p. 50) ready in advance so that you can classify (code) answers as the questionnaires are returned. All of that is straightforward because the answers are predetermined. Only their *frequency* remains to be discovered. You can also have the kinds of display worked out in advance (tables, line and bar graphs, pie charts, and so on – see Chapter 6).

5. *Less pressure for an immediate response.* Respondents can answer in their own time and at their own pace. If they want to think about their answers (or go and check on something) then they can do so. Actually this is a mixed blessing, because the expectation of a response, in an interview, can also motivate the respondent to 'work' on it.

6. *Respondent anonymity.* This is not straightforward and there are probably big individual differences. Some people will undoubtedly feel freer in an anonymous style of responding; but others may be cautious about committing themselves to paper. In small-scale research the 'anonymity' may be only nominal in character. The general consensus is that the value of 'anonymity' in encouraging respondents to disclose is uncertain. And there is one major practical disadvantage: that you won't know who has responded and who has not, and therefore to whom you should send a follow-up prompting letter – see Chapter 5.

7. *Lack of interviewer bias.* There is much evidence to show that different interviewers get different answers. Differences of perceived race, sex, social class, age and educational level all affect the answers people give (although this can be anticipated and planned for). This 'standardization' relates to the next point.

8. *Standardization of questions.* If everyone gets the same questions then it can be claimed that another source of

bias is eliminated. However, whether these questions are *understood* in the same way is another matter.

9. *Can provide suggestive data for testing an hypothesis.* Whether one calls it an 'hypothesis' or not, researchers commonly have ideas they are testing out or checking on when they construct a questionnaire. For example, a nurse may be interested in sex differences in response to advice on after-care following hospitalization. Do women follow this advice more carefully than men? If a significant difference is found then further in-depth research can be justified as to *why* this is so.

The foregoing presents a pretty strong case for questionnaires but we now need to consider their negative features (Box 2).

Box 2   Against questionnaires

- Problems of data quality (completeness and accuracy).
- Typically low response rate unless sample 'captive'.
- Problems of motivating respondents.
- The need for brevity and relatively simple questions.
- Misunderstandings cannot be corrected.
- Questionnaire development is often poor.
- Seeks information just by asking questions.
- Assumes respondents have answers available in an organized fashion.
- Lack of control over order and context of answering questions.
- Question wording can have a major effect on answers.
- Respondent literacy problems.
- People talk more easily than they write.
- Impossible to check seriousness or honesty of answers.
- Respondent uncertainty as to what happens to data.

Problems of data quality

Data quality is a problem at several levels (see below), but a fundamental problem is that questionnaires are often completed hastily and carelessly. Ask yourself: how much thought and trouble did you take over the last questionnaire you completed? And what was it that made you skate through it as quickly as possible? For these reasons one cannot have much confidence in some of the answers that are given (but you don't know which), and some questions may not be answered at all.

Even factual accuracy cannot be assumed. For example, details of an individual's medical history (When did you last see your GP? What was the problem?) are often answered wrongly, as nurses and doctors well know. If this is true for 'important' details, how accurate are people going to be about less important facts?

1. *Typically low response rate unless sample 'captive'.* In part this depends on whether the respondents know you personally, on whether the questionnaire is seen as interesting and worthwhile to complete (and when did you last see one that was like that?) and the amount of time and trouble that has to be expended to complete and return it. Surprisingly little thought is usually given to making a questionnaire *intrinsically* rewarding, but this may be a key factor. 'Impersonal' questionnaires typically attract a response rate of around 30 per cent, although follow-up requests may increase this by up to a third. Over 50 per cent has to be accounted quite a good response. A 'captive' group – students in a lecture hall, staff at a training meeting – can mean a response rate of nearly 100 per cent, but such questionnaires are slotted in between other activities. An unexpectedly poor response to questionnaires can be a salutary experience for the novice researcher.

2. *Problems of motivating respondents.* Few people are strongly motivated by questionnaires *unless* they can see it as having personal relevance, e.g. gathering information and opinions on job organization, status and salary, or related to a topic of *real* importance. The market is questionnaire saturated. Even if a questionnaire is completed and returned, few respondents will really have worked at the answers. This dimension is very apparent in a face-to-face interview (where motivation is much stronger), because you can see the effort the interviewee has to make to give a considered response.

3. *The need for brevity and relatively simple questions.* Opinions are divided as to how long a questionnaire should be, except that it should be as short as possible. Some are impossibly long. For example, one American questionnaire on experiences of childhood sexual abuse consisted of over 600 questions. A questionnaire may be *too* slight to be taken seriously, but four to six pages (depending on design and layout) is probably the maximum. In exceptional cases up to twelve pages may be feasible. The need to simplify questions, e.g. avoiding compound questions, or using jargon, is also part of the pre-piloting and piloting stages. Writing questions that are not misunderstood, that are not ambiguous or inadequate for the topic, is surprisingly difficult.

4. *Misunderstandings cannot be corrected.* Linked to the above, one of the most frustrating things for the researcher is to find that a question has been 'misunderstood'. Of course, this is largely the result of inadequate attention to the detail of questions in the development stage. However, human psychology being what it is, 'misunderstandings' can never be entirely eliminated, although careful piloting can pick up questions that are ambiguous or misleading. This is one area where the interviewer has an unarguable advantage: misunderstandings can be immediately detected and corrected.

5. *Questionnaire development is often poor.* Of course, this doesn't have to be the case, so how can it be a weakness of the technique? The answer is given in the opening paragraph of this chapter: that questionnaires are so easy to do quickly and badly that, in a way, they invite carelessness. More troublesome research methods do not necessarily lead to better quality data, as any experienced supervisor of postgraduate research students can attest. But techniques (like experimental research) which are difficult to understand and set up, even in a basic form, do have a kind of in-built discipline – which is one of their attractions. The other is the rigidity of a method that removes many uncertainties, which is perhaps one reason why those who have mastered it cling to it. That is 'hard' research; 'soft' research, like using questionnaires, is easy to do badly, difficult to do well. That is true of all methods outside the traditional scientific doxology.

6. *Seeks information just by asking questions.* Well, how else do you do it? The answer is that in a questionnaire you cannot – a major, but usually unrecognized, limitation. The alternative is the face-to-face interview – but don't you ask questions in an interview? Of course, but questions aren't the only – or even the best – way of getting people to tell you what you want to know. Questions presume that people have ready answers; there is also something controlling, because interrogatory, about a question-and-answer approach. Skilled interviewers get people to talk, to reflect on their responses, steering them in a particular direction in various ways, including, most powerfully, by an interested silence. Oblique approaches like an appreciative comment ('That must have been difficult'), expressing one's own uncertainty ('I'm not sure I understand that') or reflecting back what the interviewee has said ('you thought there was more to it than the reasons you were

11

given') have the effect of directing and encouraging people being interviewed without making them feel that they are being grilled.

7. *Assumes respondents have answers available in an organized fashion.* This is not a problem with straightforward factual questions (except for accuracy of recall). It is much more of a problem when opinions are being sought. People may not have definite opinions, or may not have reflected on the topic behind the questions, or the range of choice-answers may seem too tidy or definite. Because they feel they have no real choice people often select an answer whether they have an 'opinion' or not – although they may just fail to respond.

8. *Lack of control over order and context of answering questions.* In a questionnaire, as in an interview, questions are (or should be!) in a logical, developmental order – the same for everyone, presumably. But if questions are answered in a different order, because the respondent picks at random, then the responses are not 'developed' by the sequence. In effect, he or she is answering a different questionnaire. A further complication is that the respondent may ask other people what *they* think, or discuss the questions, perhaps radically modifying the response.

9. *Question-wording can have a major effect on answers.* A lot of research shows that apparently quite minor differences in wording or how the question is framed can produce radically different levels of agreement or disagreement, or a different selection of answers. To some extent these can be cleared up by prior piloting; another way to deal with this effect is to have essentially similar questions that cross-check the trend of the responses.

10. *Respondent literacy problems.* In almost any industrialized country around 5 per cent of the population will have difficulty with reading. In some groups (for example, the unemployed, or teenage mothers) the proportions

are much higher. Questionnaires can be simplified and usually require a minimal written response, but if your research group is likely to have literacy problems then piloting assumes even greater importance; it may be that a questionnaire is inappropriate. Many people who can read perfectly well have difficulty with spelling or expressing themselves in writing, so that a questionnaire may seem excessively daunting.

11. *People talk more easily than they write.* This is an almost universal truth. Fluency in written expression is a minority skill – and highly prized. So 'open' questions in a questionnaire are probably only appropriate for an educated, professional group – and not always then, because writing takes time and effort. If you are after depth and detail in the responses then you will almost certainly have to use a semi-structured interview: easier for the respondent, much more difficult for you.

12. *Impossible to check seriousness or honesty of answers.* People tend not to take questionnaires seriously; their answers may be frankly frivolous. And because they are impersonal, the honesty and integrity of answers may not be seen as a priority. One of the impressive things about face-to-face interviews is the extent to which people will work at giving a serious, considered response.

13. *Respondent uncertainty as to what happens to data.* We live in an information-conscious age. There is a general feeling that a lot of information about people, confidential or otherwise, is stored away on disk or paper: Even 'anonymous' information is still about *you* and may be identifiable. That's one point. The other is that questionnaires commonly do not explain *why* the information is being collected and what *use* it will be put to. Making this clear initially is part of good questionnaire construction and should not be treated as just a 'courtesy formality'; it could have a major effect on whether or not someone completes the questionnaire.

A negative picture?

The cumulative effect of these 'negative' points can seem discouraging. Well, there are cautions to be borne in mind. But they should also be seen as a list of pointers to producing a good questionnaire. Some of the defects indicated can be quite easily avoided or mitigated; a few you just have to live with. But if you are to get the best out of this research tool you need to know both the strengths and the limitations. As with many other things in life, a successful outcome is a lot to do with trouble taken in preparation.

2

Preparation

Developing a questionnaire

The logical starting point for developing a questionnaire is to ask what your broad aims are: what is it you are trying to find out? And, stemming from this: what are your specific research questions? Research papers and reports are typically written up with these aims and questions at the beginning (usually after a literature review), the teasing out of the issues and the specification of the context of the research to be reported.

But, in reality, research does not proceed in quite that 'logical' order, and those who assert that it does only have experience of research methods from textbooks. The nearest model of research to the logical order is the experiment – studying the literature, deriving research questions, setting up an hypothesis and testing it by an experiment. But even that 'scientific' model does not reflect the *psychological* order of development. 'Running' an experiment is often a late stage following on from a good deal of messy to-ing and fro-ing, dead ends and uncertainties; and the *real* discoveries are usually made at this stage – the experiment being run to demonstrate them. This is the deductive, hypothesis-testing model of research derived from the natural sciences (and correctly used where appropriate). In real-life research you can rarely run experiments for ethical and practical reasons.

You have to make sense of the evidence as you turn it up – the *inductive* model. And in this way of doing research your aims and research questions are continually being modified and redefined – in other words, the design is *emergent*.

This doesn't mean that you do not *start* at the logical point (what do I want to find out?) but that you have to clarify and redefine your aims and questions as you get to know better the people and the context you are researching. This is a perfectly respectable research process and *one where you need to keep careful records as you proceed*. Most easily and usefully this is done in the form of field notes which will include your attempts to specify your research objectives at stages in the process alongside new data, insights, hunches, observations, things you have read and so on.

When you come to write up your report, using your notes, you will be able to give an account of how your research questions emerged.

Suppose, for example, you work in industry and there is a problem of high turnover in office staff. Your broad aim is to find out the reasons for this and what could be done to change it. If there are over 200 staff at all grades then a questionnaire looks like the best general technique, probably supplemented by a small number of face-to-face interviews.

There are two key method questions:

- How do you decide on the questions to ask – both your broad research questions and the specific questions in the questionnaire?
- Do you survey all members of staff or just a *sample* of them?

Deciding on the questions

The first step might seem to be to set down the main topic areas (pay, hours of work, physical conditions, job prospects, management support, and so on) and then to put down a lot of specific questions on paper under these headings – a kind of individual brainstorming session. There is nothing wrong in that provided the process does not stop there, because it assumes that you know what the key topics or issues are for the group or 'population' you are researching. A particular danger is that your own experience may lead you into the assumption that you *know* what the issues are because you are familiar with that kind of context. For example, as a teacher you may know about bullying as an issue in a school you have worked in, but the problems and solutions there may be radically different or inappropriate in another school: bullying, like other social problems, has a lot of 'local' characteristics. The problem of *assumed* similarities is one specially to watch out for because it is a trap easy to fall into.

But what is more surprising is when 'researchers' construct questionnaires off the top of their heads for groups of people quite different from themselves. If, like the writer, you are an academic of a certain age who has spent most of his life in universities, what can you know, for example, about the working conditions of care staff in children's homes? An experienced social worker would obviously have more idea. But as a researcher one still needs to ask: how would you find out *in a question-specific form* what their concerns are? A government or social work department may well have certain headings (satisfactions/dissatisfactions, recruitment issues, career development, training needs), but these are a very general guide and may miss out whole areas of real concern to child care workers. What are presumed to be the key issues by outsiders are sometimes way off the mark even when these issues appear 'obvious'. To take another example, most single parents are known to have very low incomes. But is low income their main concern? How would you find out?

The key point is that you may not know what you should be asking questions about. Even if you are fairly sure you do, you need to check this out. And you do that by asking the people you are researching to tell you; we return to this point later in the chapter.

Deciding on your sample

Questionnaires are one of the tools of population surveys – a main research method. Surveys usually aim at a comparative and *representative* picture of a particular population. Social scientists use the term 'population' in the special sense of the group or list they are sampling from; they also speak of this list as a 'sampling frame'.

So you have a list of people appropriate to your research (if not you have to construct one). Do you ask questions of *all* the people or do you take a 'sample'?

In small-scale research, and using questionnaires, it may make sense to include everyone, especially if 'sampling' could be misinterpreted (Why was I picked? Why wasn't I asked?). If the numbers are large, running into hundreds or even thousands, the only practicable way is to take a sample.

The problem with sampling is the difficulty of making it representative. There is one sure-fire method of getting a truly representative sample and that is to use *random* or *probability* sampling. The word 'random' can cause confusion. Novice researchers often describe their sample as random in this sense – 'I picked 20 people at random.' However, this is not what is meant by a random sample: picking people who just happen to come to hand is called a 'convenience sample'. This is better than asking no one at all, but it is unreasonable to assume that the resultant data are representative.

In a random sample each individual in a given population has an equal chance of being selected: this is done by assigning a number or code to each person and then generating a sequence of random numbers or codes (rather as premium bond numbers are selected). For this to work you need to take a large enough sample so that sampling 'error' is reduced: the smaller the sample the less confidence you can have that it is representative. It is the size of the sample that counts, not the size of the 'frame' it is taken from. For example, one thousand individuals randomly sampled from ten million will correspond very closely to the larger group (and the degree of error can be calculated).

But the practical difficulties of setting up the sampling frame, generating the random numbers and getting the identified individuals to cooperate are enormous. One way round the difficulties is to use *systematic* sampling. For example, in a school you could take every fifth child from the class lists; or in the office staff sample you could select those whose names begin with certain letters of the alphabet.

More widely used as a way of being 'representative', however, is stratified *quota* sampling. To take the office staff example again, you could make a breakdown of the whole group in terms of sex, age, employment grade and location, and take a 25 per cent sample which is pro rata on those characteristics – representative in that way. If someone will not agree to take part you can add in someone else from the same category. Quota sampling is widely used in political polling, usually in conjunction with a probability/random sample of areas.

Convenience sampling we have dealt with above in defining random sampling. It is most useful when you are piloting the questionnaire and need feedback on its clarity and workability.

This is necessarily a simplified account, but with these issues in mind we can get on with the *pre-pilot* stage of questionnaire development.

The pre-pilot stage

This is the first phase of questionnaire development before you have an actual questionnaire to try out (the pilot stage –

see Chapter 4). At this point you are trawling for topics and items for inclusion and checking on those you have provisionally drafted. Collecting and analysing data at this stage can be time-consuming and needs to be kept under control, but even on a small scale can be an eye-opener. There are three main ways of doing it:

- the *focus* or discussion group;
- the semi-structured interview;
- the semi-structured questionnaire.

Depending on your research needs, you can use any or all of these techniques, but it is usually best to start with a group discussion to clarify the main areas or topics of concern.

The focus or discussion group

Here you introduce topics for discussion or ask questions of the group you are researching (nursing staff in intensive care wards, learning support teachers, children in the first year of a secondary school, and so on) and, steering the discussion, note the issues that come up, any variations and the range of views and opinions that are voiced. Here your role is that of chairperson and minute-taker. The advantages are that people can spark each other off, so it is motivating, but a few more confident individuals may dominate and it can be difficult to follow up points – although here your chairing skills come in ('I think Claire made an important point there, perhaps you could open it out a bit for us?'). In general, the results are impressionistic rather than specific, but they do enable you to get a feel for the topics of importance. And it is interesting to note how they change your own research priorities.

The semi-structured interview

This is usually better for honing in on a particular topic and also picking up specific ways of phrasing topics and questions. Writing good questions is something of an art, and one's first attempts can sound very wooden or jargonish. More respondent-friendly ways of putting the questions can well come from potential respondents themselves.

In a semi-structured interview you introduce the same kind of topics as with a focus group, but you can 'probe' and clarify more easily because you only have to attend to the one person. You will not get the same breadth unless you do a lot of them but you will get more depth.

So as to give full attention to the person you are interviewing you need to tape-record the interview (with the respondent's permission, of course). Trying to make notes is very distracting and, as you have to edit as you go, you have to make hasty decisions as to what's important.

To ensure that the analysis does not become a too lengthy or unmanageable process, you need to keep the interview moving briskly along; the most important information usually comes up at the beginning of an answer, although that is by no means universally true. Overall length should be ruthlessly kept down to 20 to 30 minutes – you will soon see why!

Analysis is easiest if carried out immediately afterwards, while memory and impressions are still fresh. The procedure is as follows:

- Run the tape right through once, listening for *substantive* statements, those that really make a point: they usually stand out.
- Have a notebook and pen ready, start the tape again, stopping when a key point comes up so that you can note it down. Replay if you are not sure of the words.
- Do a content analysis – organizing similar points into categories (see Chapter 7).

From these 'key points' some of your topics and questions will emerge.

The semi-structured questionnaire

With some groups (educated, literate) this may be the preferred technique. You ask your 'open' questions as before, but you do so with ample space for a written response. The advantages are:

- You do not have to edit or transcribe, it is done for you.
- When people write they are more economical than when they talk (most verbal interviews are mainly made up of 'fillers' and repetitions, ordinary speech being like that). Writing makes people get to the point.
- Content analysis is relatively easy – you just go through and highlight the substantive statements.
- You can get a lot of information for the expenditure of only a little effort, provided you have identified the right topics through preliminary discussion groups.

A combination of methods

All of the above methods can of course be used in combination, in which case you should use them in the order given because each one facilitates the next.

If you carry out this exercise it can be instructive to compare the topics and questions you finally decide on with the items that you put on paper initially, off the top of your head. There will be areas of agreement, but the discrepancies will be glaring. The strength of empirical research (where you go out and get your own original data) is that it is almost always a salutary corrective to what we think we know.

What about the answers?

The very term 'questionnaire' focuses you on the identification and writing of the questions. But questionnaire construction is not just about that: you also have to be clear about the probable *answers*. As most of the questions will be closed, you will, at least in some questions, have to write the answers; we deal with that in Chapter 3. What has to be borne in mind is that what you are doing is question *and answer* construction.

One of the most valuable things to come out of the pre-pilot stage will be to sensitize you to the kinds of answers people come up with (and how you have to phrase the question to get the kind of answer you intend). For example, if you are researching the take-up of medical services you might ask 'When did you last see your GP?', which might elicit a response such as 'Well, I haven't seen my GP for years but in the summer I was staying with some friends and I had these dizzy spells and they took me to see *their* GP.' That alerts you to construct questions such as 'When did you last see *a* GP?', supplemented by 'Was it your regular GP?' and further follow-up questions if they respond 'No'.

You might also find that the range of answers is so varied that you have to either turn one question into several or leave it as an open question, but avoid this if possible for economy of effort. Open questions have to earn their place.

If you have good evidence as to the probable kind and range of answers that come up you will be better placed to decide on the question type.

3

Drafting the Questions (and Answers)

General principles

Drafting the questions and designing the layout are the two key stages in questionnaire construction. They are closely linked, but this chapter deals only with the writing of the questions (and answers). These are the heart of the matter, and the design dimension (which is not superficial) is dealt with in Chapter 4.

Key topics

In your pre-pilot work you will have identified the key *topics* you want to ask about. You need to think about the layout *order* of these topics. Which should come first? Does one lead into another? Within these topics you will be writing questions which should themselves lead logically one into another. This clustering and progression will make it easier for the respondent to work through, and also make 'dotting around' less likely – a problem with questionnaires, as noted on p. 12. Further, these kind of logical sequences support and focus each question: they are not 'stand alone'. The whole thing will therefore make more sense to the respondent.

The topics usually fall into three main categories:

- questions of *fact*;
- questions about *opinions, beliefs, judgements*;
- questions about *behaviour* (what people do).

Factual questions usually come first and in chronological order. They are mainly obvious but it may be that not enough thought is given to their selection or construction. They are key in the sense that they may provide a basis for dividing up the group of respondents to see if their answers are different; for example, by sex, by age group, by educational level, by income. What you have to ask is: what use is this going to be to me in my analysis? What level of information do I need? (so don't make it more elaborate than is required).

Questions about attitudes, opinions, beliefs, etc. are the most difficult to write and the most problematic to answer. At anything more than a relatively superficial or simple level they are probably not suitable for a wide-ranging questionnaire. The reasons for the reservations are:

- People often do not have a developed opinion.
- Attitudes are often complex, so that fitting them with a question is difficult; they also vary in intensity.
- Particularly in scaled responses (*strongly agree* to *strongly disagree; very satisfactory* to *very unsatisfactory*), there is often a limited use of the scale – mainly on the mildly positive side.

Opinion questions work best when the key statement or question is phrased in a balanced and neutral way. If your question indicates the 'good' or 'correct' or 'socially desirable' answer then you are leading or biasing the respondent. Bias is not a matter of people knowing what you want to find out, but which answer you approve of.

People are uniquely well placed to report on their own behaviour (which is why market researchers give this area so much attention). Understanding it is another matter. A key point is that the question should be specific, e.g. 'Where did you last buy a tie?' rather than 'Where do you usually buy your ties?'

Complex or lengthy questions should be avoided, as they are more likely to be misunderstood or seen as inappropriate, at least to the range of answers provided.

Providing appropriate forms and ranges of answers is as important as getting the questions right. Well-constructed answers simplify the respondent's task *and clarify the question.*

A final point is to avoid unwarranted assumptions. For example,

What is your marital status?
Married   ☐
Divorced   ☐
Single   ☐

Since we live in the age of partnerships (which may not be heterosexual) this sort of question will be seen by many as exclusive, discriminatory and offensive: it doesn't fit the way people are.

Drafting the questions

Working within one topic area at a time, draft questions that fit the purpose of your research: why are you asking this particular question? You also need to ask yourself what *type* of questions you should be using (which also means what kind of *answers*). At this stage you can write more questions than you will end up using, but start eliminating questions (and pruning those you plan to keep) as soon as possible. There may be a lot of questions you would like to ask, but the real criterion is which ones you need to ask: those that you cannot do without. If you set a limit – say, no more than five questions for each topic – you will soon find that you can

27

prioritize, and then set a cut-off point. It may also be that you can combine two questions by a change in wording.

This is an enjoyable stage in the process. Writing questions is something of an art, but persistence and hard-headedness will improve one's first mediocre attempts. Scrutiny by colleagues and piloting proper will carry the process further. A well-developed questionnaire has a lean, logical look to it that is unmistakable.

Drafting the answers

It helps if you do this at the same time as writing the questions. And getting this part of it clear makes you tweak the questions so that they lead into the range of answers in an even-handed way.

One thing that has to be consistent is the style of response. Don't mix up *tick* responses with *underlining* or *circling* responses. In any case, most people are used to box-ticking, although sometimes a cross is useful to indicate a negative or 'disagreement' choice or response. As far as possible, avoid the need for writing in answers. However, the overriding rule is that it should be immediately clear what the respondent has to do. We now go on to consider the different question and answer types.

Selected responses

This is the most common form and is particularly appropriate for *factual* questions. The simplest kind is that which requires no more than a yes/no response. For example:

Do you own a car?   Yes ☐   No ☐

You *can* use simple selected responses for opinion questions or statements (e.g. 'The government is handling the economy well': agree/disagree) but these usually work better with a more graded, i.e. ranked or scaled, response (see p. 31).

In practice they are most suitable when you are asking people to give basic information about themselves (i.e. subject descriptors). For example:

Gender (*tick box*)   M ☐   F ☐

What is your age-range?   18–25   ☐
26–35   ☐
36–45   ☐
46–55   ☐
56+   ☐

You could, of course, ask people to write in their sex or age, but it is simpler this way and establishes a way of responding. When the question is a little more complicated, then providing the answer choice makes the question clearer for the respondent.

Please tick the highest level of your educational qualifications (this is a UK list):

None   ☐
GCSE (Grades D to G)   ☐
GCSE (Grade C or above)   ☐
A level or equivalent   ☐
First degree   ☐
Master's degree   ☐
Doctorate   ☐

'Selected response' questions are simplest when the respondent only has to tick one answer. However, sometimes he or she may need to tick more than one. For example:

Which of the following branded painkillers have you used in the past three months? *Tick or complete all relevant boxes.*

Brand A   ☐
Brand B   ☐
Brand C   ☐
Brand D   ☐

Other (please write in) _____
(Note that this kind of question would follow on from a simple Yes/No question i.e. 'Do you use painkillers?')

The inclusion of the 'other' category is sometimes useful as a catch-all, but it should not be used to make up for a lack of care in questionnaire preparation. In the example above, pre-piloting will have identified the 'probable' analgesics.

A selected response format can be used as an alternative to a scaled or ranked response. For example:

Please indicate which aspect of the training programme you found most useful (✓) and which you found least useful (✗).

	✓ or ✗
pre-planning	☐
presentation style	☐
visual aids	☐
evaluation	☐
promoting discussion	☐

The value of this format is that the respondent is forced to make a choice. And you might care to follow this up with an open question as to why he or she found the ✗ item least useful.

Specified response

This is a simple form of open question; it could be like the previous one but without the given choice. For example:

What was it you found *most* useful about the training programme?
Please write in: _____

What did you find *least* useful about the training programme?
Please write in: _____

Again, you could follow these up with 'Why?' questions.

Other factual questions can be of this type (where you cannot identify the range of responses). For example:

Which primary school(s) did you attend?
Please write in: _____

Where did you do your nursing training?
Please write in: _____

Ranked responses

A slightly more subtle way of getting people to express preferential judgements is to ask them to rank items in order of preference. If you are doing market research then branded products might be the items. But you could use it with the question on p.30.

Which aspect of the training programme did you find most useful? Put 1 against what you found most useful, 2 against the next most useful, and so on down to 5, for the least useful.
pre-planning ☐
presentation style ☐
visual aids ☐
evaluation ☐
promoting discussion ☐

The strength of this technique is that it gives you a better idea of the relative merits of the different items. Note, however, that it is *not* legitimate to average the 'score' for each item: the reason for this is explained in Chapter 6, which deals with data analysis.

Scaled responses

These are the ones we are most familiar with: you complete them in hotels and on flights. For example:

> How do you rate the food provided on the plane?
> Very good___ good___ adequate___ poor___ very poor___

Most scales are five points like this one; you can go up to seven or you can eliminate the 'neutral' one to 'force' a choice. There are three major weaknesses to scaled responses:

- people often don't use the whole scale (which is why a seven-point scale is usually redundant);
- people tend to be more or less positive even when it is highly doubtful that they are *really* satisfied;
- whatever response they tick, you don't know *why*.

These weaknesses are so marked that it is surprising they are so widely used. A great deal of research (see, for example, Barbara Gutek's 1978 paper 'Strategies for studying client satisfaction', *Journal of Social Issues*, **34**(4), 44–56) shows that people say or report they are satisfied when other indicators (like what they do) strongly indicate otherwise.

If the purpose of a questionnaire is to improve a service of some kind, then knowing that people are not satisfied is not useful unless you know in specific detail why. A way round the latter difficulty is to 'route' subsequent questions.

> If you rate the food provided as 'poor' or 'very poor', please briefly explain *why*.
> Write your answer here: _____

There are other ways of scaling for opinions:

> The standard of nursing care in this ward is high:
> agree ☐
> not sure ☐
> disagree ☐
> strongly disagree ☐

If you weight the scale like this you are emphasizing that you want to know about dissatisfactions. Again you can route follow-up questions for those who have expressed negative judgements.

Routing questions

It is possible to 'personalize' questionnaires so as to follow up responses in more detail and get more precise information. The examples above are a simple follow-on to a particular question. But you can be more elaborate than that. For example:

Q1. Did you feel the training programme was useful?
Yes ☐
No ☐

If YES go on to Q2, if NO go on to Q5.

Please write in your answers
Q2. Which elements did you find most useful?_____
Q3. Which element might be improved?   _____
Q4. How?   _____

Go on to Q7.

Q5. Why? _____
Q6. What do you suggest could be done to improve the training programme? _____

_____

Q7. What aspects of your professional practice do you feel were not covered by the course? _____

_____

Even in this very simple example you can see the potential for confusion. Of course, this can be minimized by a carefully designed layout, but the capacity for respondents to get lost or confused in a questionnaire should not be underrated. This is where we are up against a fundamental weakness of questionnaires – even the simplest attempt to vary or individualize or get beneath the surface looks over-elaborate. The strong recommendation is that, apart from the sparing use of a simple, optional, follow-up question, routing should be avoided.

The relationship between questions and answer type

What is readily apparent from the above is that the kind of question you ask is to some extent determined by the kind of answers you want. Obviously, 'opinion' or 'judgement' questions will require some sort of scaled or ranked response in most cases, but it doesn't have to be the case – you can use a specified open response ('What worried you most when you heard you were being admitted for day surgery?'). You need to ask: is this format the best one for what I am trying to find out?

On the whole, if you are to maintain the respondent's interest, a variety of question/answer types is necessary, so you should think in these terms as well. This is part of the design process which is dealt with in the next chapter.

Key 'open' questions

Some open questions expect and require only a simple and factual answer ('Who explained to you what day surgery involves?'). But there are some open questions which require a more free-ranging and unpredictable response. Questions like these can be motivating for the respondent, and they enable the researcher to trawl for the unknown and the unexpected. One or two questions of this type can be a good way of finishing a questionnaire, which can otherwise easily leave respondents with the impression that their personal opinions or experiences have to fit the straitjacket of prescribed answers.

The questions can be as open as you like, e.g. 'We have

tried to make this questionnaire as comprehensive as possible but you may feel there are things we have missed out. Please write what you think below, using an extra page if necessary.' Or they can be more prescriptive: 'What do you think are the positive and negative aspects of being a supply teacher?'

The analysis of these kinds of answers can be troublesome and certainly lacks the neatness and speed of 'answer-prescribed' questions. But, as was pointed out in Chapter 1, and even if you have done the pre-piloting and piloting conscientiously, there remains considerable scope for genuine discovery. The kind of content analysis required is described in Chapter 7. Essentially there are two aspects to it: reducing the substantive points made to key categories (so that you can examine them in that way) and presenting the data in such a fashion (usually by key quotations) that the flavour of the original is not lost.

Piloting the questions

Piloting the questions is distinct from piloting the questionaire, which is part of the design process.

Piloting the questions is mainly about getting the *words* right. No matter how much time and thought have been spent on developing and writing the questions, until they have been tried out on someone, you do not know whether what you mean or intend is going to be clear to those answering them.

The stages are these:

1. Prepare a list of questions and answers, *including more than you need*. If, for example, you wish to end up with no more than 30 questions, you should pilot half as many again. These can be alternatives or variants that you are not sure about.

2. As far as possible, put them in a logical developmental order.
3. Try the list out first with one or two people who are not specialist to the group you are targeting. If your target group is made up of nurses or teachers or social workers or computer programmers, these will inevitably have specialist knowledge and language. But jargon is always obstructive. Plain English is better. And your non-specialists will help you there.
4. Tell them that you are trying to get the questions right and that any suggestions they have or anything they find unclear will help you. Preferably sit on opposite sides of a table as you also need to watch them to observe hesitations or uncertainties that are not voiced. Use a copy of your question list on which to note what they tell you and what you observe. Radical and obvious – with hindsight – revisions often arise at this point. Indeed, this is often a salutary experience.
5. When you have revised your draft on the basis of feedback from non-specialists, carry out the same exercise with two or three members of a group similar to the one you are researching, but not from the actual group who will get the finished questionnaire.
6. The basic procedure is the same, except that you should also ask for any improvements, deletions or additions.
7. Now edit your list of questions, striking out those that did not work well or are redundant: every remaining question should have its own worth, its own job to do.

What you will end up with is a list of questions which are near definitive and ready to be part of a designed format. Further revisions will be necessary, but they will be mainly of detail.

4

Designing the Questionnaire

Design and detail

At this point it is tempting to ease off, to regard the job as all but done or even to think that 'it will do'. It surely won't. If we take an analogy with mechanical engineering, we have something that runs fairly well at the bench with you keeping an eye on it, adjusting it and understanding how it works. But putting it to practical use, in a real-life setting where it has to fend for itself, is another matter. Design and field trials are necessary to toughen it up. 'Design' means two things:

- how things *look* – attractive, accessible;
- how things *work* – whether, in a robust sense, they do what they're supposed to do.

The 'visual packaging' of your product may put people off or invite them to look into it, but it also needs to lead people into correct or appropriate use. The functional aspect of design is critical: whether it really works or whether it goes wrong.

What is this questionnaire all about?

Questionnaires are usually sent out with a covering letter of explanation which often gets mislaid and would be best incorporated in the questionnaire. Whether this is the case or not, the questionnaire should still speak for itself, in two ways:

- by its title and by what else is written on the face sheet;
- by the nature and organization of the questions – their purpose should be obvious.

If respondents are clear about what you are trying to find out and why, they are much more likely to respond appropriately and helpfully or, indeed, at all. There is a curious convention that if you tell respondents what you are trying to find out this will 'bias' them. It might simply make them more helpful. If you are mysterious about the purpose of the questionnaire they may be disinclined to answer or misunderstand the purpose, and so bias their answers in that way.

Your questionnaire title is key. For example, on the face sheet you should have a title like:

IMPROVING ACCIDENT AND EMERGENCY SERVICES

This should be followed by a few bullet points that expand on this briefly. For example:

Dear_____

- You were recently an outpatient at St George's A & E Department.
- We want to know how you found the service you received.
- This will help us to improve the working of the Department.
- Please complete this short questionnaire and return it in the enclosed s.a.e., if possible before __/ __/ 2007.
- Your reply will be treated as confidential.
- Thank you for your cooperation.

Yours sincerely

Amanda Smith
Staff Nurse

Incidentally, it helps if the addressee's name is handwritten and the letter signed by 'Amanda Smith'. And note that 'confidential' does not mean 'anonymous'.

Not all questionnaires are going to have the obviously worthwhile quality of our example here, but you need to think hard about what kind of information is going to inform the respondents and motivate them to complete the questionnaire.

It may be, for example, that the content of the questionnaire is of interest to *you* because you are working for a higher degree, but it may not be intrinsically rewarding for someone else. If we suppose that you are investigating teachers' attitudes to punishment (a topic that will interest some more than others), it will probably encourage them to respond if you explain that you are doing this as part of a master's degree dissertation: teacher colleagues will understand that that is important to you.

Layout and organization of the questions

Modern software makes it easy to produce an attractive, professional-looking questionnaire. But it is important to aim for a clean uncluttered look (don't mix too many or use too fancy fonts). However, the key to an uncluttered look, where what is required is clear, is to have plenty of space for the questions. And since the overall length of a questionnaire is critical (four to six pages is the usual tolerance maximum), one can see why the need to ensure that every question earns its place has been a recurrent theme.

Try to use a variety of different types of question/answer styles. It is extremely boring, for example, to answer a series of scaled-response questions; and people stop thinking about what they are doing.

With different question formats it is unlikely that you can

get more than six questions on a page (and sometimes fewer than that). Try it out and see. You have to include:

- the questions (numbered in sequence);
- the answers, with their appropriate boxes;
- the *coding column*.

This last is not strictly necessary but it can make the analysis (at least of closed questions) easier. Simply, as each *question* has a number, so does each *answer*, and there are more answers than questions.

For example, if we take the age-range question on p. 29, it might look like this:

			Research use only
What is your age-range?	18–25	☐	7
	26–35	☐	8
	36–45	☐	9
	46–55	☐	10
	56+	☐	11

Each possible answer has a separate number in sequence; this can be referenced to the question, if necessary, e.g. 3.7, 3.8, 3.9, 3.10, 3.11.

What you do with this coding (and the more complicated issue of coding responses to open questions) is dealt with in Chapter 7. The point here is that you have to decide on the inclusion of a coding column at the design stage. And such a column takes up that valuable commodity, space.

Doing a paste-up

Before you go into the laborious process of 'designing' your questionnaire on the computer, it is worth taking your list of questions and answers and making a mock-up by setting the questions out on the page, appropriately spaced with a coding column handwritten in. You do this as a scissors and paste job, laying out the questions, and moving them around, before you stick them down – literally hands-on. If you lay the separate pages out on a large table you can then see what your fundamental layout problems are. Mostly that means making further decisions about what questions or topic areas could or should be deleted.

A typical weakness of the novice researcher is to try to include not just too many questions but too many topics. You may find that to keep the length down you have to sacrifice either questions or a topic (or two). If retaining all the topics is going to mean that the question coverage is thin, then you should consider dropping a topic.

When you have made these painful decisions you can then use your paste-up version as a guide for word-processing your draft. A small detail here, but one that will save much confusion as you prepare successive drafts: date (and perhaps number) each draft. It is very irritating to pick up a draft and not know which one it is. Incidentally, it is also a good idea to keep copies of successive drafts in a manual file, for reference.

The first draft

This is a rewarding stage – like seeing the proofs of a book. But, as with a book, there have been so many bitty changes of content and order, quite apart from the operator defects of word-processing, that it will need careful proof-reading. Proof-reading one's own productions is extraordinarily difficult: because you know what is supposed to be there, you tend to fail to see errors, omissions and inconsistencies. Some people are especially good at it (English teachers, for example), so get someone like this to proof-read for you.

You are now ready for piloting proper.

41

The pilot study

The first stage is like the piloting of the questions. Ask two or three people (of a similar group to those who will get the real thing) to go through it while you watch and are there to deal with queries. You will need to watch very carefully because the untested element is the layout, and you may be able to observe the uncertainties here. When your guinea-pigs have done this ask for any general comments or questions they have.

Surely it is right by now? Many car designers, or developers of new drugs, have probably said the same thing at a similar stage of development. But what you find in the sort of trials when the expert is there to supervise what is going on is different from what happens in real-world conditions. Particularly if your questionnaire is going to be part of a large-scale survey, then field trials are essential, and even those are not the last word.

A proper pilot study is one where you simulate the main study. It will involve fewer people, but they will be of the same kind as your final target group. Here the questionnaire has to stand on its own feet. You send it out, and you wait to see what happens.

It cannot be emphasized too strongly that until you have done this you do not know how well your questionnaire works. Two things that tell you are:

- a low, or very slow, response rate – people don't bother with troublesome questionnaires;
- 'misunderstandings' of what a question means or how they are supposed to respond.

The first of these speaks for itself, although you might care to try out follow-up letters (see Chapter 5). The second is more difficult because misunderstandings are not always apparent. Indeed, they may only be signalled by a response which reflects a gross misunderstanding. Other indicators are:

- omitted responses;
- incomplete, crossed-out or ? responses;
- frequent comments such as N/A or extra points added to your list.

Analysing the returns

You may find it useful to do the sort of analysis you will be carrying out as part of the main study (see Chapter 6) because this can indicate areas or questions that need expanding or strengthening in some way. This will also start you thinking about the patterns of results you might expect to get. But the main analysis at this point is when you go through each return noting indicators that a question (or its layout) is problematic. By preparing a summary sheet you can note the number of the question and then list the apparent difficulties as you find them. The root cause will usually be obvious, but sometimes you will have to interpret to some extent. If the respondents are not anonymous then you can ask the individuals concerned.

The detailed refinements lead to a new draft, which must itself be carefully proof-read; all changes are potential sources of new errors. But in the end it is there: you just have to run off the copies, staple them together, and your questionnaire is ready to go out.

5

Getting Them Out and Getting Them Back

Sending questionnaires out is one thing; getting them back is quite another. It can be a demoralizing experience to send out a hundred questionnaires and, a month later, to find that fewer than thirty have been returned. It is not just a matter of the number being low, but of not knowing what the difference is between those who have responded and those who have not.

Here are the basic rules for maximizing the return:

1. The first, and overriding, consideration is one we have already dealt with: producing a well-designed questionnaire where the purpose is clear.
2. Personally delivered questionnaires (for example, to colleagues) have a good chance of being returned: they are doing it for you.
3. The greater difficulty arises when the approach is impersonal: questionnaires mailed to people you don't know (and who don't know you).
4. An important aspect is that of sponsorship and identity. Who is this person asking these questions? Where is he or she from? Teachers and nurses, for example, might be chary of answering questions that they think might get back to their employers. If your research is backed by a university or other independent research organization it is a good idea to make this clear (by using headed paper).

People recognize that such institutions are independent and non-political (in the widest sense of the term) and also that they have a certain status. Note, however, that sponsorship can have a negative effect. I recall a questionnaire sent out with the support of a government department to psychologists which their professional association stopped them responding to. This problem was compounded by inadequate piloting of professionally sensitive questions – always a point to watch. In any case, you need to make your own exact status clear.

5. Whether you are hand-delivering or mailing the questionnaire, use good-quality envelopes, with the name and address typed. Make sure that you get the person's name name, initials and preferred title right. Those sent to women should be titled Ms unless you know that they prefer another form. Getting the names right is a curiously neglected point; many people are extremely sensitive about this and it does convey an implication of carelessness. It is no use handwriting in a name on a covering letter (to 'personalize' it) if the name is wrong. I once received a letter (an invitation to speak) which began 'Dear Bob Graham ...'. It did not receive a reply.

6. Mailed questionnaires should be sent by first-class post. Some writers on the subject suggest that letters should be stamped, not franked. But a letter from a university with the university franking on it carries its own imprimatur. In any case, enclose a stamped addressed envelope – a big factor in getting a response, as many mail order companies appreciate.

7. For surveys that are intended for individuals at home, Thursday is the best day for posting – people usually have more time at weekends. Letters to organizations should go out on Mondays or Tuesdays (if only to ensure that people receive them in time to complete them that week).

8. Avoid mailings at holiday periods or when organizations

are likely to be closed, or exceptionally busy (schools at the beginning or end of term, for example).

9. Even if the questionnaires are hand-delivered, it is probably best to ask respondents to post their replies. Other forms of collection (collection boxes in a school, for example) are flawed in various ways – security and confidentiality, perhaps. A completed questionnaire is rightly seen as personal.

How long do you wait?

Some people respond very quickly, but the picture at the end of about ten days will give you some idea of what kind of response you are likely to end up with. Allowing for late returns and responses to follow-up letters, what you have received after ten days will be about half of what you can expect to get back. This is a rule-of-thumb measure but it can give early warning that things are not going well.

Give it another week and then start follow-up letters: these can increase returns by as much as a third of what you have received to date, so they are well worth the effort. However, like all elements in successful survey research, the composition of the letter requires careful thought. The following points are key:

- don't be too apologetic about prompting;
- emphasize the importance of the study *and of their contribution*;
- don't imply that you have had a poor response (imply the contrary, if anything);
- enclose a further copy of the questionnaire and another stamped addressed envelope 'in case they did not receive or have mislaid the original one'.

There is often a good response to this kind of follow-up, but it is worth going a stage further by waiting another ten days and then sending another prompting letter. A few more will arrive in response to that.

Some large surveys do several follow-ups, but the law of diminishing returns applies and you can get the negative effect of nuisance value. In summary: follow-ups are worthwhile but should not be overdone.

An inquest on the response rate

A response rate of more than 50 per cent from a sample who are not known to you has to be reckoned reasonably satisfactory. A high response rate is testimony to your questionnaire's development and the perceived importance of what you are doing. That, in itself, is a significant outcome of the research. Very well-designed questionnaires on important topics can attract responses of over 90 per cent.

If your achievement is much less than that – less than 30 per cent, for example – then the value and validity of your method and results are in question. You may have to face the tough decision as to whether you should go back to square one and use a different method.

For example, you could use your questionnaire as a recording schedule, i.e. something that you administer verbally (and there are advantages in this, as indicated in Chapter 10). If you suspect that the topics were too subtle or too sensitive for a questionnaire, you should consider using semi-structured interviews (see the companion volume *The Research Interview* in this series).

However, if the gloomy prospect of redesigning your research programme is not necessary in your case, then we can proceed to the exciting (and arduous) stage of analysing the questionnaires that have come in. Chapters 6, 7 and 8 deal with different aspects of analysis.

6

Displaying the Results for Analysis

The first stage of analysis is essentially a descriptive one: setting out the results in a summary form (tables or graphs) so that you can see the overall response to individual questions at a glance. Much of this level of analysis you will use in your final report, but it is also a stage leading on to further analysis.

Initially this stage only applies to closed questions, questions where the range of answers is specified. Open questions, even quite simple ones, require a lot more work to achieve an adequate descriptive analysis. For the moment we put these to one side as they are dealt with in Chapter 7. You will soon see why closed questions are the preferred option wherever possible.

You have two basic kinds of questions.

First, there are those that 'describe' the people who have completed the questionnaire: gender, age, occupational category, income level, educational level, and so on. These are called *subject descriptors* – categories chosen because of their probable relevance to the topics you are asking questions about. The value of this information is that it will enable you to divide up the answers to the research topic questions that come later. It is worth saying here that subject descriptors should not be chopped too finely, especially if numbers are not large. Two categories usually provide a robust division: manual/non-manual, graduate/non-graduate, annual income $\pm$ £ 25,000, and so on. Chapter 8 deals with the kinds of statistical analysis that will enable you to test the significance of the differences in the pattern of answers divided up in this simple fashion.

Second, there are those questions that provide data on the topics you are investigating – the 'meat' of the questionnaire, as it were. You start by setting them out. Subsequently, you can divide up the answers according to the different categories of respondents, to see whether there is a 'significant' difference: Chapter 8 again.

Preparing the displays

For all sets of answers there are two basic stages:

- Counting the answers ticked, using tally marks or any other simple form of checking. If you have coded the answers then you use this shorthand as your heading.
- Preparing a numerical table, or line or bar graph, which displays these results in summary form. Most people find a visual display such as a bar graph easier to read than a numerical table (see, for example, Figure 6.1).

Further, if you set out your subject descriptors in this way you can often see where the range of answers might be divided in two, with reasonable numbers above and below the line, for later statistical analysis. You may decide to incorporate these simple divisions (by age, gender or whatever) into your initial display of the answers. Nothing is lost in doing so and it may save time. Gender, in particular, is a factor which can be built in at the first-stage analysis.

Once you have done the simple analysis of your subject descriptors, a clearer picture of the kind of sample you have will begin to emerge. It may be that you will know enough about all the people who were sent questionnaires to be able to say whether those who actually responded differ radically

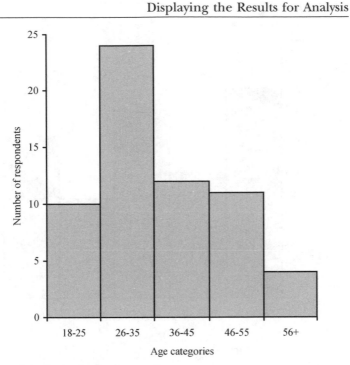

Figure 6.1 Example of a bar graph.

as a group (by gender or by seniority, for example) from those who didn't.

Analysis by question and answer type

Selected response questions

These are fairly simple to analyse when only one answer has to be selected. They are not quite so simple when more than one answer can be checked.

For example, if we take the painkiller example on p. 29 we could:

- count the number of times each identified brand (and the 'other' category) was checked (Figure 6.2);

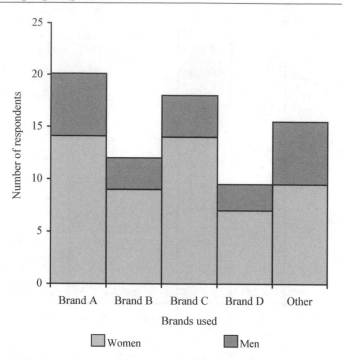

Figure 6.2 Use of brands of analgesic by women and men.

- count those individuals who only used one brand, as against those who used two or more (Figure 6.3).

To display this we might also include the gender of the respondent. From Figure 6.2 it seems that women use painkillers more often than men – this is something for later statistical analysis.

If we were interested in 'brand fidelity' we might lay out the data as in Figure 6.3. From this it looks as though women are much more 'brand faithful' than men.

But what about those who didn't check *any* boxes? The picture that emerges from Figure 6.4 is that women seem more likely than men to use painkillers. Again, this is something for statistical analysis.

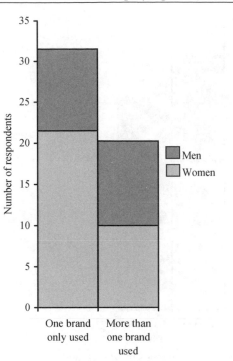

Figure 6.3 Use of one brand or more than one brand of analgesic by women and men.

At this point one can begin to see the value of simple display analysis. It sets you thinking about further questions you need to ask of your data. Are there age or social class differences, for example? Are there age × gender differences, i.e. do older men differ from older women more than younger women do from younger men? Incidentally, there is evidence that *in some respects* younger men and women are closer in habits and tastes than their elders.

When you have used the selected response format as an alternative to a scaled or ranked response (see p. 30) – asking people to identify the most/least useful or the best/least liked or whatever – the main information is likely to be found in the

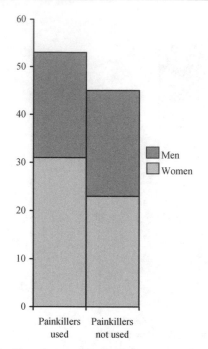

Figure 6.4 Use of any analgesics by women and men.

total picture, without further subdivision by subject descriptors (see Figure 6.5). This gives quick feedback. Note that a further open question could take this information a stage further by clarifying reasons for the judgements.

Specified responses

Specified responses (see p. 30) require a simple form of content analysis and so are dealt with in Chapter 7 as a lead-in to that slightly more troublesome topic.

Ranked responses

Ranked responses (p. 31), where answers have to be ranked in order of preference, are deceptive because numbers are

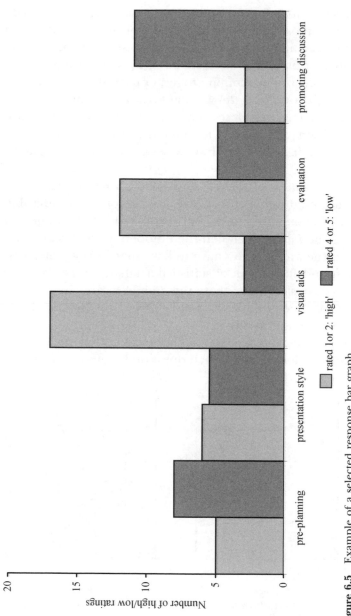

Figure 6.5 Example of a selected response bar graph.

involved (1 to 5, for example). However, all the numbers do is to *label* those items which are most or least valued. It is a relatively simple matter to note against each answer the number of times they are ranked 1, 2, 3, etc. You can simplify the picture by lumping together each item as ranked 1 or 2 (high) or 4 or 5 (low). That gives you a similar picture to the selected response items and can be used to cross-check them. If you want to show the pattern of ranks for each item it is best to draw a series of mini bar graphs (Figure 6.6).

One weakness of ranked responses is that because numbers are used rather than words it is tempting to think that you can *average* the ranks. But this is not a true numerical scale (The *intervals* between the numbers are not *equal*) and to get true averages you have to have that sort of scale. This may sound like a finicky statistician talking but it is more commonsensical than that: the numbers are, in fact, no more than descriptive words like 'high' to 'low', and you cannot 'average' words.

The answers to scaled responses can often be lumped together if, for example, each question relates to one aspect

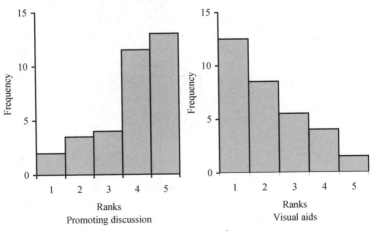

Figure 6.6   Ranked response mini bar graphs.

of the standard of service – whether it relates to the service a college provides to its students or the service you get from an airline. Suppose, for example, that students were asked to rate separate aspects of a lecture course on a five-point scale from 'very satisfactory' to 'very unsatisfactory'. You could analyse the responses as in Figure 6.7.

While this gives some indication of where strengths and weaknesses lie, it tells you nothing else, and the picture can be contradictory. Further open questions or follow-up interviews or discussion groups would be necessary to elucidate the basis for the judgements. Questionnaires can be good at providing large-scale descriptive information; they are much less satisfactory at providing explanatory data. Chapter 12 discusses how questionnaires can lead in to other research methods.

Using percentages: a caution

'Averages' and 'percentages' are what are known as *descriptive* statistics: they describe what you have in your data in a rather more tidy form. But you have to be aware of their limitations. We have already mentioned that you cannot average ranks in ranked responses. That may seem a somewhat technical argument. But for a simpler reason percentages are more easily misused. The great weakness of percentages is that you don't know (or see immediately) what the absolute numbers are. You should always ask: *a percentage of what number?*

Pie charts (see Figure 6.8) are a very good way of displaying percentages and of comparing different groups or changes over time. However, you should not use more than about four slices of the pie or it will quickly become hard to read. It is also very easy for visual displays of percentages to be misleading.

Let us assume that we have carried out a survey of nurses

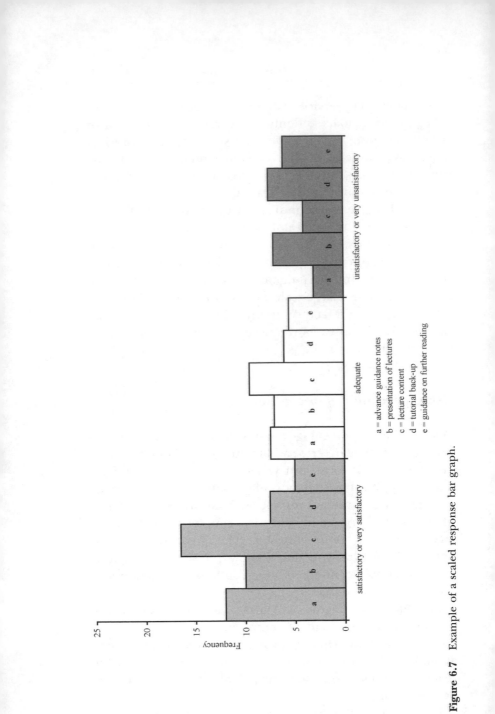

Figure 6.7 Example of a scaled response bar graph.

58

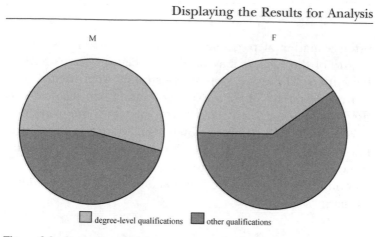

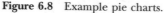 degree-level qualifications ■ other qualifications

Figure 6.8 Example pie charts.

and their qualifications in a general hospital. They can be divided into those with a non-graduate or graduate basic training qualification and those with or without special post-initial training qualifications. We find a different pattern for male and female nurses (see Figure 6.8; note these are fictional data).

From this it appears that about 55 per cent of the male nurses have degree qualifications, as compared with some 35 per cent of the female nurses. But we are not comparing like with like: in the original data there are only 30 male nurses and 250 female nurses. There are actually many more female nursing graduates than male ones.

In this sort of instance you have to consider whether percentages, especially displayed in a simple visual format, are likely to misrepresent the true picture.

What about computers?

There is a range of software which can be used for analysing questionnaire data. For very large surveys these programs can be useful, although because coding and analysis are often a matter of personal preference or the idiosyncratic nature of the data, it may be that special programs have to be written. There are similar constraints when analysing a more modest set of data. Keying in data can also be very time-consuming, particularly if you are not a fluent user.

For small-scale studies (which usually means those with fewer than 200 subjects) the basic analysis is more easily done with pen and paper and a pocket calculator, with the computer used to prepare the text and graphics in readable format.

Errors and omissions

All the foregoing presumes that respondents have completed the questionnaire correctly. In practice, answers are sometimes missed out or not filled in correctly. This is where a lack of proper development and piloting of the questionnaire comes to haunt the researcher. Respondents will sometimes go wrong even when great pains have been taken. A carelessly produced questionnaire can lead to a set of results where many returned forms (or some answers) are of little use. If you have skimped on development this is where justice catches up with you.

If the responses are not there you can only record what statisticians call 'missing values'. Incomplete or missing answers should be noted in your research report: they reflect on the evaluation of your research. Sometimes incorrectly completed responses can be 'interpreted', i.e. you can see what the respondent was trying to say. A high proportion of missing responses or unusable returns *has* to be reported in your write-up, if only because it reflects on the likely quality of the 'correctly' completed questionnaires.

Description and interpretation

This process is dealt with in Chapters 7 and 8. But let it be repeated here that the strength of a questionnaire is in description, not explanation. 'Interpreting' results and suggesting what they 'mean' is a temptation that questionnaires expose you to. At most they can suggest lines of further enquiry. If questionnaires are over-used as a method it is partly because they provide deceptively simple data which are easily over-interpreted.

7

Content Analysis of Open Questions

We need to remind ourselves here that open questions are those where the *answer* is open. The question indicates what you want to know but it does not provide a predetermined choice of answers. As will soon become apparent, the great advantage of specifying the range of answers to the questions is that, in effect, the respondent does the analysis for you.

The simplest kind of open question is one that specifies the response exactly, e.g. *Where did you do your social work training and to what level?* There will be a variety of different answers to this kind of question, and the job of content analysis is to reduce them to manageable and meaningful categories (otherwise you will have a very long list).

But you should ask yourself (at an early stage in the development of the questionnaire): is an open question really necessary and does it justify the work involved? The use of open questions can simply reflect a lack of thought or care in development; trouble comes afterwards. If the stages of question identification and piloting are carefully carried out, the range of response categories may be identified so that an open specified response question can be changed into a closed selected response one.

But if we assume that it has to be an open question, then you have two judgements to make about categorizing the answers that you get:

- What categories do they seem to fall into?
- What categories are going to be useful or necessary for your research purposes?

These overlap, but they are not the same. The basic principle is to have as few categories as possible without doing violence to the data, and while still having enough for the purposes of the research.

The first stage is to decide on the categories. And the first step in this is to list the responses you have received. If we assume that these are brief and many of them are the same, you can adjust your list, using a check mark for repetitions. Even as you're doing so, you will find tentative categories forming in your mind, though you have to keep this process in check; we humans are categorizing animals (and that includes our prejudices).

For example, having listed the responses and looked through them, you might find that the following categories suggest themselves (and would be adequate for research purposes):

- training on the job, no formal qualifications;
- social work diploma;
- degree plus postgraduate diploma in social work;
- degree in social work;
- master's degree in social work.

You can then go back to your list and check off each response under the category heading. If you want to keep track of where an individual's response is located, assign each individual a number. If you do that you will be able to do further analysis according to other data (sex, age, and so on).

Two problems with answers to open questions that make classification difficult are:

- respondents sometimes don't give you all the information you have asked for (for example, they might tell you where they trained, but not to what level);

- some responses don't fit easily into the categories you have extracted (for example, someone may have a degree but no formal training; will you put her in the category 'training on the job, no formal qualifications'?).

In practice, even the most direct forms of content analysis involve a good deal of to-ing and fro-ing and there are almost always some loose ends, unclassifiable elements which have to be reported as such.

Complex answers to open questions

There are degrees of openness in open questions. The more specific you are, the less the variety of the answers. However, if the question is wide open you may find it impossible to reduce or categorize elements of the answers. Consider the following open questions:

- How do you think working conditions for nursing staff on acute wards could be improved?
- What do you think about working conditions for nursing staff working on the wards in your hospital?
- What do you think about working conditions for nursing staff?

The differing degree of openness is apparent – and that will affect the answers you get.

How do you decide? The answer is in your response to the question: what do I want to find out? Your question should be framed to meet that without constraining the range of answers. You have to keep your own values, assumptions and judgements out of it.

The content analysis of an extended written response to a question is something you learn by doing. By starting at a relatively simple level you will be better equipped to cope with the more difficult stuff (for example, the content analysis of verbal responses to questions in a semi-structured interview; see *The Research Interview* in this series).

An exercise I have used with postgraduate research students is to ask them to write down what they see as the positive and negative features of their course. If you can do something similar with some colleagues or fellow students ('What are the positive and negative aspects of teaching in this school?') you then have the material for doing a practice content analysis of all those individuals' written response. Don't be too ambitious: around ten is ample to begin with.

'Content analysis' is one of those phrases that tend to bemuse people. Once you have done the exercise, even at the basic level suggested here, it becomes a practical activity but an intellectually demanding one: translating your material into a manageable and comprehensible form.

To attempt your very first content analysis only at the point where you are doing your main research study is a recipe for disaster, not least because practice in the exercise will lead you to make changes in your questions (and the number of open ones), but also because you will have a much better idea of what you are letting yourself in for.

Doing the exercise

Let us assume you have your set of written answers to a question of the kind suggested above. The procedure is as follows:

1. Take each person's response in turn.
2. Go through each one, highlighting *substantive* statements – the statements that make a key point, that really say something. In written form this will be true of most of the material, so your job is to separate them out. However, when you are working on the transcript of a recorded interview it is more difficult because speech has a lot of

'redundancy' – repetitions, irrelevant material, digressions of one kind or another.

3. As you mark out the substantive statements you will find categories forming in your mind. Note this process but don't do anything about it at this stage.

4. Take a break, reflecting on what you have just done. This is to give your impressions a chance to settle, without becoming too fixed.

5. Now comes the more difficult, creative stage. Go back to the beginning and, going through the highlighted statements, try to derive a set of categories. Give each category a simple heading (e.g. 'lack of feedback on performance', 'inadequate library facilities' or whatever). To begin with, just list these categories. You will get a lot from the first set of answers, more from the next, but progressively fewer as you work through them all – because individuals will be making many essentially similar points.

6. Now look at your list of categories and ask yourself whether some of them could be combined under one heading or, alternatively, split up. As you are compiling the list you will sense that some of the headings you have noted down are not adequate or appropriate in some way.

7. Go through the set of responses again, with your list of categories beside you, checking each statement against the category list to see if it has somewhere to go. Place a question mark by those statements you cannot readily assign to any category. Modify the wording of the category headings (or revise them entirely) so that they fit the statements better or can now include question-marked statements. Add new categories if necessary. When you have done this you will have something like a workable list.

8. Enter your categories in an analysis grid like the one shown in Table 7.1. The category headings go along the

Table 7.1 Analysis grid for content analysis.

Categories

Respondents	1	2	3	4	5	6	etc.
1							
2							
3							
4							
5							
6							
7							
8							
9							
10							
11							
12							
etc							

top, the names or code for the respondents down the side. In this exercise it might make sense to have two separate analysis sheets, one for positive and one for negative statements. It is a good idea to make the analysis sheets very large (at least A3 size); you will see why below.

9. Go through the sets of answers, assigning each one (where possible) to a category. Answers you cannot assign have to be dealt with separately – if only as unclassifiable. Put the *number* of the category against the statement on the original written answer: this tells you that you have entered it, and where it has gone. On the grid you can either tick the relevant box (this person made a statement that fits this category) or write in the actual statement (which is why you need space). Doing this has a lot to recommend it: it brings the summary category to life, conveys the range of answers that come under it and provides material for the qualitative analysis that comes later. Even if you tick the box where respondents and categories intersect, you should make a note of examplar quotes for each category. Survey categories have a bland, uniform quality and you need to be able to bring them to life.

10. With your analysed data on the grid you can now see it clearly enough to write up the analysis of the answers to that particular question. You write this up in two ways: as a *qualitative*, i.e. descriptive, interpretive, analysis of what people said, and as a *quantitative* (count) analysis, e.g. levels of agreement or disagreement. These differences of opinion may be related to different categories of respondent so that you can carry out a categorized statistical analysis (Do women have a different view of the course from men?). Chapter 8 deals with quantitative analysis, specifically the use of *chi square*.

11. Writing up the findings requires some interpretation, i.e. what sense is to be made of the responses to the

question. The important thing here is to balance contradictory findings. If you cannot classify a number of statements or they are unique, general conclusions or interpretations are suspect.

A final point: you will now see why the use of open questions is cautioned against. Their analysis involves a great deal more work. The bonus is that you may make real discoveries.

8

Statistical Analysis of Closed Questions

This is a chapter that many people will feel is not for them; the very phrase 'statistical analysis' will have closed their minds. Overcoming this negative attitude in students is a familiar problem for anyone teaching a research methods course with even a minor statistical component.

In part, this is because books on statistics – even those claiming to be 'basic' or 'introductory' – seem to be littered with complex algebraic formulae interspersed within a jargon-ridden text. People take fright and go to great pains to avoid any contact with this fearful topic. The problem is not helped by the fact that gifted mathematicians and statisticians are so much at ease with their medium that they cannot see what the problem is for others.

The non-mathematician can make only limited use, and achieve only a limited understanding, of statistics. But within those limits there is useful knowledge to be gained, in particular, practical tools that will help you to make better sense of your data – to say more, and to say it validly.

This chapter concentrates on only one statistical test – chi square – which deals with what are known as *categorical* data (data that fall into groups or categories) and enables you to say something more definite about the differences that appear between these different categories.

To take a practical example: in Chapter 6 we suggested (in hypothetical data) that there might be a difference between men's and women's use of analgesics (whether there is or not is a matter for research). But let us assume that in a questionnaire that included a question on whether or not the respondent used analgesics (95 questionnaires returned), 53 of the respondents were women and 42 were men. The summary results are shown in the following *contingency table* (so called because one 'variable', a source of difference or variation, i.e. use of analgesics, may be *contingent* on the other variable, i.e. gender).

	Uses analgesics	Does not use analgesics
M	22	20
F	31	22

From this it looks as though women are more likely to use analgesics than men. Don't the results speak for themselves without any statistical manipulation? Well, there is a numerical difference, but does it really amount to anything? The numbers are not very large so you would not expect an exactly identical pattern for men and women to appear. Perhaps the difference is trivial and just a chance result of the sample obtained. If you interpret the difference as meaningful, perhaps you are making claims that the data will not bear. It is easy to exaggerate a difference that is not really significant, and significance is something that statistics can give you a precise value for. The less likely it is that a difference could have occurred by chance, the more significant it is.

By using a statistical test to check on your impressions (whichever way it goes) you can extract more meaning from what you have found. It may be that you have uncovered a difference that requires further research, in particular why there is this difference. For example, you could conduct semi-structured interviews and/or produce a further questionnaire that explores that topic in more detail. See the discussion on multi-method approaches in Chapter 12.

The rationale of chi square

The basic premise of chi square is quite simple. In the contingency table on p. 72 you have the actual or *obtained* frequencies. How far are they from the *expected* frequencies if there is no difference between men and women?

Out of the total number of people involved (95), 53 use analgesics, that is 55.8 per cent. If there were no difference between men and women then you would expect 55.8 per cent (23.4) of the men and 55.8 per cent (29.6) of the women to use analgesics.

So what you get in comparison is this:

	Obtained		Expected	
	Use	Non-use	Use	Non-use
M	22	20	23.4	18.6
F	31	22	29.6	23.4

Because the totals for both tables have to be the same, once you have worked out one category (or 'cell') the other is fixed or determined. This difference between the *obtained* frequency (o) and the *expected* frequency (e) is the basis of chi square.

We can now go on to calculate it for this example.

Step 1

For each cell calculate the difference between the obtained frequency (o) and the expected frequency (e). The formula for this is written as (o − e).

For the first cell in the top row you have $22 - 23.4$, so you have a minus answer (-1.4). For the second cell you have $20 - 18.6 = 1.4$. Note that the numbers are the same, but one is negative, the other positive. Quite simply, if there are fewer men using analgesics than expected, there must be correspondingly more who do not. If we take the first cell in the second row we get $31 - 29.6 = 1.4$ and in the second row $22 - 23.4 = -1.4$.

All the numbers are the same but half are positive and half are negative. This is because once *one* difference is determined in a 2×2 contingency table such as we have here, all the rest follow on. This is known as *one degree of freedom* (1 df), a notion you need when you come to use tables for reading off the significance level for a particular chi square result.

The more rows and columns you have, the more degrees of freedom (df) you have. The formula is $(r - 1) \times (k - 1)$, i.e. the number of rows (r) minus one times the number of columns (k) minus one. In a 2×2 table that is $1 \times 1 = 1$ df, as has already been explained. If we had a 2×3 contingency table – for example, if there were three levels of analgesic use (regular users, occasional users, non-users) – then we would have $(2 - 1) \times (3 - 1) = 1 \times 2 = 2$ df. And so on. For most practical purposes, and certainly for smallish numbers, a 2×2 table is often all that is practicable.

Back to our calculation. We have these differences:

	Users	Non-users
M	−1.4	1.4
F	1.4	−1.4

Step 2

To get rid of the negative signs you square each difference $(o - e)^2$. This gives us:

74

	Users	Non-users
M	1.96	1.96
F	1.96	1.96

Step 3

Divide each number by the *expected* frequency for that cell (o − e)^2/e. For example, for the first cell in the first row we calculate $1.96 \div 23.4 = 0.084$. For the second cell in the first row it is $1.96 \div 18.6 = 0.105$. And so on. We end up with these results (all taken to three places of decimals):

0.084	0.105
0.066	0.084

Step 4

If we add these up we get the value of χ^2 (this is the Greek letter 'chi'), which in this case is 0.339. To find out whether this is statistically significant or not you need to consult a table of chi square values, which looks something like this:

df	0.70	0.50	0.30	0.20	0.10	0.05	0.02	0.01
p *values*								
1	0.148	0.455	1.074	1.642	2.706	3.841	5.412	6.635
etc.								

From this table you can see that our result falls between chi square values for $f = 0.50$ and $p = 0.70$, and we can say right away that it is definitely *not* significant.

The chi square value you actually find is unlikely to be *exactly* one of those in the table: it is going to be either higher or lower. In this case the chi square indicates a p value *less* than 0.7 but *greater* than 0.5. You can say, then, that $\chi^2 = 0.339 = p < 0.7$ or > 0.5, where $<$ means 'less than' and $>$ means 'greater than'. But what, you may ask, is a p value?

This is the kind of detail that many statistical texts treat as obvious. But if you are completely new to the subject you will need to work through an explanation.

1. 'p' stands for 'probability'.
2. Probability is most easily understood in terms of how often (one in ten, one in a hundred, etc.) a given result could occur by chance.
3. The less often the result could occur by chance the higher the probability that your result is significant.
4. Statisticians talk about 'levels of significance' in these terms.
5. In statistics p values are usually expressed as a decimal of *1*. Once you get used to it this is a very economical way of expressing probability. For example:

> 0.5   = 5 chances in 10, or 1 chance in 2 (evens)
> 0.1   = 1 chance in 10
> ---
> 0.05 = 5 chances in 100 or 1 chance in 20
> 0.01 = 1 chance in 100
> 0.001= 1 chance in 1000
> and so on.

Below the line results are conventionally judged as more or less 'significant'.

To fix this in your mind, do the following exercise (answers given at the end of the chapter):

What are the probabilities for these significance levels?

0.25 = 1 chance in ___
0.2   = 1 chance in ___
0.02 = 1 chance in ___
0.005 = 1 chance in ___
0.0001 = 1 chance in ___

There is a simple pattern, even if initially you are a bit blind to it!

If we now go back to our χ^2 result of 0.339, which doesn't even reach the $p = 0.5$ level, we can see why it is emphatically not significant. It could easily have occurred one time in two by chance alone. Now this is interesting, because if we had just relied on our 'eyeballing' of the data on p. 72 we might have found ourselves saying that 'women are more likely to use analgesics than men', when chi square tells us that for the numbers we have the difference is definitely not significant. It is not statistics that lie but the impression you can get from differences between small numbers. It is easy to read into your data something that is not there.

A practical exercise

You may feel you have followed all this through and understood it. But you don't really understand a procedure until you can do it.

Let's assume that in the questionnaire on the use of analgesics (where we found there wasn't a significant sex difference between those who used them and those who didn't) we get the following results for brand fidelity:

	One brand only used	More than one brand used
M	9	13
F	22	9

Calculate chi square following the procedure already given (answer at the end of the chapter).

Limitations on the use of chi square

If the *expected* frequency in any cell of a 2×2 table is less than 10 you have to apply a correction (known as Yates's correction). We won't go into that here, but you need to be aware of that limitation. If expected frequencies are less than five in any cell in a 2×2 table you should not use chi square at all.

If obtained frequencies are very small (mostly less than 12, for example), chi square is inappropriate and you should use *Fisher's test of exact probability*. You would need to consult a specialist statistical text for this. In itself it is not difficult to understand, but it involves the computation of *factorials* (the factorial of 10 is $1 \times 2 \times 3 \times 4 \times 5 \times 6 \times 7 \times 8 \times 9 \times 10$). Factorials are written as 10! and so on, and since Fisher's test involves multiplying factorials you soon get into very big numbers indeed. This means you would have to use a computer with specialist software such as SPSS (*Statistical Program for the Social Sciences*). Don't let that discourage you. If you get results that are small but extreme they may well be significant. For example:

M	11	1
F	2	9

A statistics specialist, or indeed anyone fluent at using SPSS, would be able to run this for you very quickly.

Answers

p values

0.25	= 1 chance in 4
0.2	= 1 chance in 5
0.02	= 1 chance in 50
0.005	= 1 chance in 200
0.0001	= 1 chance in 10,000

Chi square

$\chi^2 = 4.788$.
What is the p value?
Is it significant?

9

The Use of Questionnaires in Surveys

Surveys are a main method in social research; and questionnaires the instrument most commonly used, although face-to-face or telephone interviews have their place.

We briefly outlined the use of surveys on pp. 18–19 while the parallel volume *Small-scale Social Survey Methods* provides a comprehensive coverage. The present chapter serves as a bridge to that, and chapters 10 and 11 show how the same basic questionnaire can be employed as a structured interview.

Why do a survey?

There is no one all-purpose method in social research. Each has its strengths and weaknesses, hence the emphasis on multi-method approaches in Chapter 12. But what are the particular qualities and uses of surveys? Almost by definition a survey takes in the wider scene; it is both more comprehensive and more representative than studying individuals – allowing breadth rather than depth. One of its main uses can be to indicate where a more focused investigation should take place. It also provides a context for such micro-studies.

A comparison is a geological survey searching for oil deposits. In broad terms geologists would know where such deposits might lie, but the area is vast. A survey asks more specific questions: samples of soil and rock are taken and analysed; test drillings are made, many of which will be found to be unproductive. However, some sites will be identified for a full-scale drilling investigation: an expensive process which may or may not produce a yield that justifies the cost. But without the preliminary work the cost would be even greater, and the results correspondingly disappointing.

In social research we can think we know what these productive areas might be, and we can easily be wrong about that. More importantly we may miss a promising area because we haven't looked widely enough, we haven't surveyed the scene.

Surveys as a corrective device

'Prejudice' is a term with its own (pejorative) flavour: racial prejudice, religious prejudice and the like. We don't like to think we are like that, yet in fact we are all a mass of prejudices. It is very difficult, probably impossible, to approach anything with a completely open mind. Everything is prejudged, in the sense that we have a limited existing knowledge and a set of expectations, however tentative, of what we are going to find.

A survey where we take note of the findings is a corrective to those entirely normal prejudgements. To take an example: if in an academic institution you are appraising and developing taught Master's degree programmes you have to know the needs and difficulties of students entering these programmes. Experience is, of course, a big help here. But it is also a blind spot, in that you may not see things because you don't know where to look, or don't think there is a problem.

A naïve eye may see more: so in research we need to develop the 'naïve eye'. A systematic survey of students and, from a complementary perspective teaching staff, may yield some surprises. At the time of writing I have been undertaking just such a survey. Within that we have identified for curriculum development the topic of searching for, using and evaluating academic journal papers. When we interviewed individual students, supervisors and specialist library staff we found that even where students had identified such papers, they were not confident about analysing them in relation to their own research topic, or critically evaluating what the papers contained. In a word the problem was one of *assimilation*. A first stage was to get students to summarize these papers (which meant that they grasped the essence) and then, in individual tutorials, to critically discuss the methods, findings and conclusions. Only through this process did they come to absorb what was in a particular paper.

A strategy for real-world research

In real-world research a survey is commonly part of a practical strategy:

- broadly identifying an area for investigation
- systematically appraising the wider field
- identifying topics for focused investigation
- identifying issues for practical action
- implementing changes
- evaluating those changes.

This kind of problem-solving strategy is sometimes described as *action research*: a term that has been around for some time and has in consequence became both slightly stale and overextended. But it gives research a direction – why you might carry out a survey in the first place. The question then is: *what are you going to do with the results?*

Producing useful results

The basic requirements are:

- having a clear purpose in your questionnaire design
- having topics that are well focused to this end
- ensuring a representative coverage of the survey population.

As indicated on p. 48 a low or even a modest response rate may mean considering alternatives to a postal questionnaire, or alternatives to this as the sole data-collecting instrument. The key question here is whether the group which has responded is substantially different from the population as a whole. If you have identified the potential participants on the basis of their fitting a *quota sample* (where categories of individuals are selected in proportion to how similar people appear in the group being sampled) and the balance of respondents is similar, then an assumption of representativeness is reasonable. Where there is a marked difference between the pattern of those who have responded and the balance in the quota sample then the method may not be fit for purpose. In that case you may have to take the option of face-to-face interviews where you can build up your sample, one person at a time, according to the quota you have decided on.

If the sample is not one of cross-sectional representation but is based on same-category characteristics (qualitative representiveness) such as users of particular software, owners of motorcycles or fathers who are denied access to their children, then any judgement as to how acceptable the obtained sample is has to be based on other criteria – data scarcity, or the problems of getting a supplementary or replacement group. In either case, the difficulties have to be acknowledged and a reasoned justification given.

Anticipating the problem

These last points raise the issue of whether a questionnaire is an appropriate instrument in the first place. *If you cannot afford to lose any from your sample you should consider interview alternatives to questionnaires from the beginning.*

The argument for these is best stated by taking the inverse of the box on p. 8. What are the advantages of interviews?

- Superior data quality (completeness and accuracy).
- Better response rate.
- Easier to motivate respondents.
- Questions can be expanded or explained.
- Misunderstandings can be corrected.
- Control over how questions are answered.
- Question wording can be adjusted.
- No problems with reading questions.
- For respondents talking is easier than writing or less effort.
- Judgements can be made as to the seriousness or integrity of answers.
- The use of the data obtained can be explained as necessary to those being questioned.

The same questionnaire for all purposes

If you decide to employ interviews does that mean that the development of a questionnaire has been a waste of time? On the contrary: a verbally administered questionnaire (which is all a structured interview amounts to) has precisely the same pattern of development and only slight variations in what is presented.

In effect only the mode of delivery is different. Apart from the advantages listed above, it is the ability to *compose* your sample according to a quota that can argue in favour of a face-to-face presentation. With a questionnaire the sample is 'composed' by those who choose to respond and it is likely to be impossible to redress any imbalance in the quota. On the other hand, carrying out interviews is time-consuming, which means going for a smaller sample size than with a questionnaire; but even if the numbers are smaller the overall balance will be better.

There are different rules to carrying out interviews, different details to take into account, but they don't amount to much. We consider them in the next two chapters.

10

The Face-to-Face Questionnaire: Recording Schedules

If there is one argument for face-to-face live questionnaire interviews it is that cost-conscious market research companies favour them. Shopping-street interviewing of this kind is part of our everyday urban experience and one cannot but admire the dogged persistence of these front-line market researchers. They are nearly always women because approaches from the female sex tend to be more acceptable and less likely to be avoided. Of course there are many refusals but with a steady flow of available shoppers that is of little consequence. The interviewers scan those who stream past them identifying people who (a) look willing and (b) fit their assigned quotas. One can learn something from observing them, not least the speed of operation (the term 'feverish haste' sometimes applies).

What they are doing is composing their sample; and they will keep going until they achieve it because they are paid by results.

The issue of valid generalization

In a good restaurant the wine waiter will draw the cork and sniff it; he will then swirl some wine in a glass and sniff that. What he is doing is checking whether the wine is 'corked' – whether the cork has failed in its function of keeping the air

87

out so that the wine has become oxidized. This is a sampling technique: estimating the whole from a part of it. Although the term may seem a rather grand one for a swift professional action, the wine waiter is carrying out a process of *empirical generalization*, estimating the condition of the whole bottle of wine from fractional evidence. To do that the sample has to be representative.

The great virtue of what we call *recording schedules*, after Moser and Kalton (1986), is that they enable you to compose a sample (pro-rata to the wider population you have identified) which will have a reasonable claim to reflect the character of the whole. True, not every one approached cooperates but the solution is under your control.

Adapting a questionnaire

The content of a recording schedule is the same as a questionnaire: the difference lies in the detail of the mode of delivery. One dimension requires special attention and that is *duration*. In an on-the-street situation where you are dependent on the goodwill of the people you accost, they obviously cannot be kept standing for any length of time: ten minutes is a just about tolerable maximum. But as recording schedules are commonly used (and are useful) with people who are busy, and during the working day, a similar duration is likely to be all that is practicable and acceptable in any setting. Making these short periods productive is the ultimate test of efficiency in the design and administration of the schedule.

Recording the responses

A postal questionnaire has to do all the work by itself: you aren't there to speak for it. In a recording schedule the written responses are recorded *by the researcher*, the respondent has to answer a spoken question or indicate a choice from a card (known as a *show card*) which gives a range of answers. Because the actual recording schedule is just for the researcher who is working at speed it can be much more summary and 'bare bones': indeed, the more so the better. It just has to be quick, clear and error free. The elements are:

- the question the interviewer has to ask.
- the prompt to produce the relevant show card (SC1, SC2, etc.)
- a simple way of recording the answers (e.g. circling a letter for the choice made).

Using show cards

Since this is the only content difference compared with a postal questionnaire, it needs to be described in some detail. It might seem paradoxical to give people things to read when you are having a face-to-face interview but there are good reasons for this. Here is an example of a TV preference show-card.

> SC1 *Question*: Please look at this card. From **a** to **j** which is your favourite kind of TV programme?
>
> | | | | |
> |---|---|---|---|
> | **a** | News/Current Affairs | **f** | Travel |
> | **b** | Comedy | **g** | Culture/Arts |
> | **c** | Reality TV | **h** | Soaps |
> | **d** | Sports | **i** | Quiz Shows |
> | **e** | Drama | **j** | Natural History |

It would be tedious to read out the whole range of choices and people might 'lose the place' and have to ask you to repeat it. When people are being asked to make a choice comparison then a show card has the advantage of simultaneity – all the choice elements are there at the same time (see the examples given on p. 29). These formats also act as a prompt or reminder (one of the virtues of multiple-choice question-and-answer formats). In this way the recording schedule combines the advantages of a printed questionnaire with the advantages of a live presentation.

'Picture' show cards

A show card is not necessarily in text form. We live in a visual age and responsiveness to images in one form or another is part of contemporary culture. You can, of course, use such visuals in a questionnaire but they take up a lot of space and it is often difficult to steer respondents through the desired sequence.

It is here that show cards with a sequence of images, presented live, work much better. You can pass them across the interviewee's field of view rapidly, with your voice as a prompt to what to look for. Identification, comparison and choice are the main elements. For example:

- Can you put a name to any of these faces?
- Do you know what any of these logos stand for?
- Which of these modern paintings do you prefer?

– and so on.

Apart from the kind of information they yield, visual show cards add variety to what can be a rather plodding experience.

Open questions in a recording schedule

Open questions, that is where the *answer* is left open, have only a limited place in a questionnaire and even on a modest scale pose problems, and will certainly involve a great deal of work at the level of analysis as Chapter 7 demonstrates.

Including them in a questionnaire can be a valuable exercise but the quality of response is often very limited. People may be happy, or at least willing, to race through a questionnaire ticking boxes. Writing out the answer to an open question requires a different level of effort. Most people talk a great deal more easily (and fluently) than they write. This is nothing to do with being literate; simply that speaking is a much more practised skill than writing (even if most talking says very little).

Fluency apart, a 'live' open question is more motivating because of the personal dimension. It is also supported in the sense that the person being interviewed gets guiding responses from the interviewer. These are as much non-verbal as verbal (what is sometimes referred to as 'active listening').

Interviewees can be very voluble at the end of a structured question-and-answer session so *recording* can be a problem. Scribbling away while they're talking may be all that's possible in an on-the-street situation; otherwise a tape recorder is strongly recommended – you can get a lot of material in just a few minutes.

Even on this limited scale you gain an insight into an important difference between interviews and questionnaires: that the latter seek to get information just by asking questions and there are limitations to this way of finding out what people think. Although the 'open question' variety may start off as a question, the treatment is more of the character of encouraging people to develop their responses. What they have to tell you is often not organized in a neat 'answer' format: subsequent analysis is largely a matter of extracting and categorizing the substantive elements from the narrative flow (speech has a lot of 'redundancy' in this respect).

These elements, as well as the pre-coded responses to closed questions may well indicate the need for complementary methods of data-collection as discussed in Chapter 12, not least more extended, loosely structured interviews where issues that have emerged can be explored in greater depth and detail.

11

Using Questionnaires in Telephone Interviews

The structured format of a questionnaire is well suited to interviewing by telephone, but the technique has its own particular character.

The rise of the telephone interview

The universal possession of a telephone in Western society is mainly a phenomenon of the last 50 years or so, the pace of acquisition having accelerated with the emergence of mobile phones of decreasing cost and increasing efficiency (along with their desirability as multi-function fashion objects). Together with television, computers and the possession of a car they are seen as almost the basic requirements of contemporary living, with usually only the very poorest in our society not having at least some of these.

In social survey terms this means that almost everyone is accessible by phone; not to be so is almost regarded as eccentric. However, the fact remains that a survey using telephone interviews excludes those who are *not* accessible in that way. Poverty is not the only reason but it is the usual one, and this may be important.

In 1936 the US magazine *Literary Digest* reported on a telephone survey of some four million voters at the time when Franklin Roosevelt was up for re-election as President.

On the basis of the results obtained it was predicted that he would lose when in fact he won with a large majority; the simple reason being that, despite the size of the survey, it excluded non-telephone owners and it was among these groups that Roosevelt had overwhelming support.

Now this happened a long time ago but the point remains: any survey that depends on communication accessibility is biased to the extent that a part of our society is not on tap in that way (perhaps a lesson for polls that rely on email responses). Postal questionnaires, at the very least, depend on people having a fixed address (or any address at all). We haven't the space to consider this further, but it is worth pointing out that within our self-consciously organized society, of which surveys are a part, there is still an 'under-class' whose style of living – usually described as 'chaotic' or 'disorganized' – makes them difficult to access, and hard for the rest of us to understand.

The telephone interview as a contemporary nuisance

The expansion of cold-call sales approaches parallels the development of similarly unasked-for market research interviews. The scale of the problem has led to schemes which allow telephone users to exclude most such calls (in the UK the Telephone Preference Scheme).

The prevalence of this contemporary nuisance means that telephone interviewing in general has become 'con-taminated'. Books on telephone interviewing, mainly American, have extensive coverage on the topic of over-coming what is termed 'resistance', advocating techniques of a facile subtlety that would hardly deceive a six year old. If you're planning to use telephone interviews you need to put as much distance as possible between how you use them as a bona fide researcher, and this all too typical experience – a form of harassment.

The ethical dimension

In the context of what has been recounted above it can be seen that the use of telephone interviews poses ethical questions for the academic researcher. Of these consent and clear information of what is being requested is the bottom line; and the request has to be presented in such a way that a refusal is accepted without demur.

If basic agreement to being interviewed is obtained then the next step is to consult the convenience of those involved: *when* and *where* it would be best to call them. It must also be made clear *how long* such an interview will last; this must be an accurate limit and one that will be kept to.

Many people cannot be telephoned at work because of the nature of their duties (teachers or nurses, for example). Those working in shops or with domestic care responsibilities may be similarly constrained because of necessary demands on their attention. So it is essential to make an appointment just as if you had to meet for an interview. And when you make the call you should check that it is *still* a convenient time: busy people often experience unpredictable changes in demand.

The advantages of telephone interviewing

The main advantage is that the interaction is 'live' and immediate, having some qualities of a face-to-face interview except for the most obvious one. This means that misunderstandings can be clarified and cues picked up from tone of voice, hesitations and the like.

Note that telephone interviews are made much easier if the schedule is sent to the respondents in advance, so they have the questions in front of them as a further, visual prompt. *You* complete the corresponding schedule of course, but doing it this way means that the person being interviewed does not have to give strained attention to your voice alone. This makes for a more relaxed, supportive style of interviewing. You can get through the 'closed question' material quite rapidly; and as with a face-to-face recording schedule the main benefit in terms of *content* is in the response to open questions.

The most simple advantage, which may be a critical determining factor in some research projects, is that people can be interviewed anywhere in the world that is accessible by telephone. Such a study is likely to involve more 'advantaged' groups, perhaps individuals of high status. Even language is not usually a barrier at this level because of the increasing internationality of English. The only restriction may be to consider time differences – and the convenience of people whose time may be heavily committed.

The disadvantages of telephone interviewing

The main disadvantage is a corollary of the main advantage listed above. Although the interview is 'live' you cannot see the person you are interviewing and vice versa. So all those non-verbal elements which are part of normal communication are missing: it is perhaps this which makes telephone interviewing such hard work (and so limits the duration). It remains to be seen whether videophones – still in the future for most of us – will make much of a difference. My experience of video interviewing suggests that much of importance will still be lost, not least that elusive interpersonal chemistry so vital to achieving empathy.

It is for these reasons that the telephone is not well suited to the less structured kind of interview where the process of engagement and responsiveness to the person being interviewed is a fundamental dimension of its successful operation. It *can* be done but the skills required only come from long practice. Unstructured or semi-structured interviewing (i.e. composed of open questions) also poses the problem of recording the responses. You get some indication of this if you have a few open questions in your structured schedule. Anything more than a minimum number of such questions may mean that you would have to use specialist telephone recording equipment (standard for market researchers). There are two issues here: *cost* – around £150 in the UK – and *ethical considerations*, as people need to be clear that they are being recorded and why.

A brisk pace is part of the character of a structured telephone interview. This is partly to maintain the momentum of the interaction but it also conveys the message that the respondent's time is not being wasted – the approximate duration of the call should have been specified in advance anyway. And sending a copy of the printed schedule means the respondent can follow the progress of the interview. One of the irritating qualities of telephone calls in general is that they can appear indeterminate, that you are pinned down by a voice coming through the ether.

A final point

A neglected element in telephone interviewing is that of *social closure*. In a face-to-face situation there is no equivalent to terminating an interview as putting down the receiver. That conveys an abrupt message which may be quite unintentional. A conscious effort is sometimes needed to express your thanks; to explain what you plan to do with their interview and with the research project as a whole; as well as offering to send a summary of the project's findings.

Such 'leave taking' will not be as protracted as in a face-to-face interview but some attention given to this stage leaves an entirely different impression from a brusque 'now I've finished with you' cutting off the interaction.

12

Questionnaires as Part of a Multi-method Approach

Questionnaires are rarely sufficient as a research method on their own. Indeed, that is true of every method, especially when you are dealing with a complex, real-world situation. There are several dimensions to an adequate picture of any human activity. Different methods have different, even if overlapping, strengths and weaknesses. If you use a range of methods you can put together a more complete picture. The *case study* exemplifies this approach (see *Case Study Research Methods* in this series).

When you have analysed the results from your questionnaire you will see its limitations. What you have is a standardized, descriptive set of data that raises more questions than it answers. In particular, *why* did respondents select these answers? Why is there this difference between one group and another? And so on. In addition, results from a questionnaire have a thin, abstract quality, rather remote from the reality of people's lives. What is it like to be a staff nurse in a busy general hospital, or a teacher in a rural comprehensive school, or a care worker in a children's home?

If the basic research questions are complex (when are they not?) then your data are going to look pretty thin and superficial if all you can report are the results of a questionnaire. In a small-scale study this lack is going to be particularly apparent.

Surveys that employ questionnaires will often include what

are known as *archival* data (information from written records: staff turnover, changes in the level of job applications, increases in the number of single parents, staff absences and so on; whatever is available and appropriate to provide a context); and also, and in particular, the results of semi-structured interviews with a small number of those who answered the questionnaire. Indeed, questionnaires sometimes end with an invitation to volunteer for an interview.

The need for further methods providing different kinds of data will become apparent when the questionnaire research has been carried out. You will see that you need to do background research on some topics: policy documents, work records, government legislation, departmental regulations and so forth. Even more clearly, you will see which topics or questions could usefully be developed and explored in detail in a semi-structured interview. If you want to convey a picture of the reality of people's lives and, more importantly, what their questionnaire responses might mean, then a face-to-face interview is without parallel as a method. In other words, it doesn't just *illustrate*, it also *illuminates*.

What does 'semi-structured' mean? If you look back at Table 1.1 on p. 3 you will see where it stands on the structured-unstructured continuum. You have clear questions you want answered, but you ask them in a way that invites an open response; you prompt the interviewees when necessary and you have to keep them on track and keep them moving. There are good reasons for this. Uncontrolled (or *under*-controlled), an interview can soon run to an hour and a half, or more (and may not be on the topic).

The problem is not the time spent doing the interview: it is the time spent transcribing it and the time spent analysing it. You can reckon that a one-hour interview will take ten hours to transcribe, and five hours to analyse ... if you are good at it.

If you think that your questionnaire could or should be

complemented by interviews you should study the companion books in this series (especially *The Research Interview*). Again, don't rush into it. The under-prepared interview is a time-consuming disaster without parallel in research methods.

If this all seems daunting, remember it is quality, not quantity, that counts. Three or four carefully prepared and carefully analysed interviews lasting half an hour each can bring your research study to life. A simple ratio of one interview for every ten questionnaires is quite a substantial back-up. But you have to judge what you can manage.

You can also select people according to their representative characteristics for the group, or focus on a particular sub-group whose (minority) answers have raised special questions that need to be explored.

The potency of interview data is even further enhanced if you have video-recorded the interviews. There are various reasons for doing this, discussed in *The Research Interview* cited above. But quite simply it adds to the vividness of the verbal content of the interview by providing the non-verbal dimension of communication. This can be important if you intend to present your findings mainly in lecture or seminar form (see Chapter 13). The point here is that you can intersperse the relatively dry, factual data gleaned from your questionnaire analysis with the video interview expansion on what these results might mean. However, it is important to select the most focused sections of the video material (perhaps only two or three minutes at a time). Video can easily run away with you, so that the presentation loses, rather than gains impact. Obviously, the making of these recordings, and their use, has to be with the permission of those involved.

If interviews are so much trouble, are they worth it? Aren't people more likely to give information in a questionnaire where they don't have to face up to someone? It depends on the specific interaction – how the interviewee perceives or gets on with the interviewer. But what evidence there is

101

suggests that people are often cautious about what they put on a questionnaire form, especially material that is of a personal nature. For example, one study of women's experiences of sexual abuse in childhood, with all of them first completing a questionnaire, found that the sub-group interviewed reported incidents they had not disclosed in the questionnaire. You can trust an interviewer, you cannot 'trust' a questionnaire. And putting personal things on paper is like letting a part of yourself go, you know not where. Interviews seem to gain in depth *and* validity.

A multi-method approach to research has the potential of enriching (as well as cross-validating) your research findings, but it is more difficult to blend all of this together in a coherent report. Presenting your research findings is the focus of the final chapter.

13

Presenting Your Findings

A common experience of those who supervise research students, particularly those who are pursuing a degree by thesis only – a rather solitary business – is that it is at the writing-up stage that they stall. There are a number of reasons for this: research weariness (it can be a long haul), a drop in motivation as earlier excitement wears off, the complexity or apparently indeterminate character of what has emerged. It may seem strange that, having gone to all the effort of collecting the data, people delay writing up or even abandon their thesis altogether. But it happens. There are two main reasons:

- pulling all the material together to make best sense of it is an intrinsically difficult task – the most intellectually demanding of all;
- people are diffident about writing, about putting their understanding or interpretation forward.

But analysis and writing up is a stage where real discoveries are made. Isn't that a paradox? Surely you have made your discoveries in the data? But data do not speak for themselves: they have to be coherently analysed and, within the limits they will bear, interpreted. You have to make what connected sense of it you can. You have to describe and explain what you were trying to do, what you have found and how you understand it so that others can see for themselves.

And in making it clear for them, you are making it clearer to yourself. Many a teacher has discovered that.

This is no extended consideration of the writing process: a fuller treatment of that topic is to be found in the last chapter of *Case Study Research Methods*.

Who are you writing for?

And, it could be added, to what end? It is helpful to think in terms of different *levels* of presentation, of different audiences.

Level one is the extended full report, often as a post-graduate degree thesis, which must follow institutional regulations as to length, format and stylistic conventions. Many reports at this level are remarkably difficult to access, as I have good reason to know. You plough through them, asking time and time again: what is all this about? As the person who wrote the report *you* may feel you know, but you still have to make it accessible to others. And in fact, if it isn't readily apparent to the reader, it is probably not crystal clear to you.

If someone were to ask you, 'What is your research about and what did you find out?', you should be able to give a coherent answer in five minutes:

- what the background was;
- what the questions were;
- how you investigated them (methodology);
- what results you obtained;
- what you think your results might mean (theory or explanation).

If you can't do this you aren't in a position to write up, for the simple reason that the way in which you give your report a structure when writing is dependent on your having a clear basic structure in your mind.

Level two involves boiling down the essence of your study into a chapter in an edited volume (unlikely if you are a novice) or a journal article (usually around 4,000 to 6,000 words). Perhaps you haven't thought about publication; if you haven't already published you may feel that it's not your sort of thing. But if you have some interesting findings (and some interesting things to say about them) then publication is something you should seriously consider. Research is about adding to knowledge; in a small way you may have done that, and it is only by publication that you can make your research available to others. After all, you benefited from reading what other people have done.

By publishing, of course, you are opening your research to critical scrutiny: that can be uncomfortable, but it is an important part of the process of becoming a researcher. The better research journals have their papers *refereed*; that is, they are sent to, usually two, independent referees who provide anonymous critical feedback. The results of this process may make you grind your teeth (referees sometimes misunderstand what you meant or were trying to do – but whose fault is that?). But there is something to be learned from all criticism.

Before you submit a paper to a journal you should study carefully the 'Notes to Contributors', which are usually on the inside back cover. These specify preferred content, format, conventions, length and the like. Your paper may not even be considered if it doesn't follow these rules.

Refereeing is a process that takes weeks, even months. The editor will then write to you:

- rejecting your paper;
- accepting it;
- or, more usually, asking you to resubmit after you have responded to the referees' criticisms.

Quite apart from the pleasure of seeing your work in print, an offprint of your paper is a good way of distributing your findings in summary form (and it carries a certain cachet if it has been published).

Level three is the communication of very summary findings, perhaps on no more than one to two sides of A4.

People like feedback, especially if they have helped you in some way (given you access, advised you and so on). And it may be that the people who completed your questionnaire or agreed to be interviewed would also like to know the outcome. It is a conventional courtesy to indicate this on the questionnaire or at the time of the interview. *And if you say you are going to do it, then make sure you do.* There is a French proverb: the wise man always does what he says, but does not always say what he does.

Level four is giving a live presentation. Your summary (level three) will be useful here as a handout, as well as providing the basic structure, but a live presentation greatly enhances it. Like the face-to-face interview it communicates more powerfully: it is richer. You have the dimension of interaction: you can sense misunderstandings, deal with queries, vary your pace and emphasis. Keep it brief: a half-hour is probably a maximum, followed by questions or discussion.

A Powerpoint presentation of key points (a prompt for you as you are talking, as well as your audience) is valuable. But it should be very summary: the kind of thing that can be read almost at a glance.

If you can add, as indicated above, even just five minutes of carefully selected, carefully edited video, you could make a powerful impact. Aim for quality, combined with a focused clarity of structure.

Endnote

One of the things that always comes out of presenting your findings is that you learn more from people's reactions, questions and criticism and thus gain new insights into what you have done. And a clearer idea of what further research might be necessary or worthwhile.

Recommended Further Reading

C. A. Moser and G. Kalton (1986) *Survey Methods in Social Investigation.* Aldershot: Gower Publishing.
ISBN 1 855 21472 5.

First published in 1958, this book has a reprint history which is the envy of all textbook authors. Although in many respects out-of-date (it antedates the widespread use of computers), it is uniquely comprehensive and reflects a level of understanding and breadth of experience that has no parallel in written form. Some of the content is highly technical but don't let that put you off. Most of it is written in a straightforward style, with a level of detail that warrants careful attention.

C. Robson (2002) *Real World Research: A Resource for Social Scientists and Practitioner Researchers* (2nd Edition). Oxford: Blackwell.
ISBN 0 631 21305 8.

This ground-breaking book is a comprehensive presentation of research methods appropriate to, and usable by, practitioners. It is this that marks it out from the competition. An indispensable resource, attractively written.

Index

accuracy 9
action research 83
advantages of
    questionnaires 5ff
aims of research 15ff
analysis 7, 43, 49ff, 66ff, 91,
    103ff
anonymity 7, 39
answers 12, 13, 22ff
archival data 100
artefacts of method 4
attitude/opinion
    questions 26

behaviour questions 26ff
bias 7

case study research 99
Case Study Research Methods
    99, 104
categorization 49ff, 64ff,
    71ff, 91, 96
chi square 69, 71ff
closed questions 4ff, 7, 71ff
coding 40

cold-calling 94
collection of
    questionnaires 47
completion 9
computer analysis 59ff
confidentiality 39
content analysis 21, 35,
    63ff, 100
context of response 12
contingency tables 72
convenience sampling 18
'cost' of questionnaires 5ff
covering letter 38

data quality 9ff
defects of questionnaires
    8ff
degrees of freedom 74
delivering
    questionnaires 46
descriptive statistics 57
design of questionnaires
    37
development of
    questionnaires 11, 15ff

109

display of data   50ff
drafting answers   28ff
drafting questions   27ff

email   94
emergent design   16
errors/omissions   60ff
ethics   95, 97
experimental research   11, 15

factorials   78
factual questions   26
field notes   16
first draft   41
Fisher's test of exact probability   78
follow-up   47ff

gender   52ff
generalization   87–8
graphs   7, 50
Gutek, B.   32

hypothesis testing   8, 15

images   90
inductive model   16
interpretation   61, 69ff
interviewing   11, 13, 85ff, 87ff

Journal of Social Issues   32

layout of questionnaire   39ff

length of questionnaires   10, 39ff
literacy   12ff
Literary Digest   93

market research 87, 94
misunderstandings   10, 42ff
Moser and Kalton   88
motivation   10
multi-method research   2, 81, 99ff

numerical scales   56

obtained and expected frequencies   73ff
open questions   5, 13, 34ff, 57, 63ff, 90ff, 96–7
organization of questions   38ff

'paste-up' draft   40ff
percentages   57ff
pie charts   7, 57ff
piloting questionnaires   42ff
piloting questions   35
Powerpoint   106
practising chi square   77ff
practising content analysis   66ff
pre-pilot stage   19ff
presentation of findings   104ff
probability values   76, 79

pruning questions   41
publication   104ff

qualitative analysis   69
quantitative analysis   69
question development
   16ff
questioning   11
quota sampling   19, 84ff

random sampling   8
ranked responses   31, 53,
   54ff
recording schedules   48,
   87ff
refereeing of journal
articles   105
report writing   16
Research Interview, The   48,
   66, 101
research questions   16
response rate   9, 42ff, 45,
   47ff
Roosevelt   93–4
routing questions   33

sampling   16, 18ff, 84ff,
   87–8
sampling error   19
satisfaction, measures of   32
scaled responses   31ff, 53
selected responses   28ff,
   51ff
semi-structured
   interviews   20ff, 100ff

semi-structured
   questionnaires   22
showcards   89–90
significance, statistical   8,
   53, 71ff
*Small-scale Social Survey
   Methods*   81
social closure   97
specified response   30ff, 54,
   63
sponsorship of
   research   45ff
standardization of
   questions   7
statistical analysis   50, 52,
   71ff
subject descriptors   49, 50
surveys   18ff, 46ff, 81ff,
   93–4, 99
systematic sampling   19

table of statistical
   significance   75
telephone interviewing   6,
   93ff
Telephone Preference
   Scheme   94
telephone recording
   equipment   97
thesis   104
title of questionnaire   38

video interviewing   96
video phones   96
video-recording   83

wording of questions   12
writing questions   25ff
writing up research   103ff

Yates's correction   78